Practice Book

GRADE 3-2

Harcourt

Orlando   Boston   Dallas   Chicago   San Diego

Visit *The Learning Site!*
www.harcourtschool.com

Contents

JOURNEYS OF WONDER

Coyote Places the Stars 3–10

Why Mosquitoes Buzz in People's Ears 11–17

A Bookworm Who Hatched 18–26

Cloudy With a Chance of Meatballs 27–36

The Crowded House 37–43

Leah's Pony 44–52

The Three Little Javelinas 53–61

Cocoa Ice 62–72

Yippee-Yay! 73–81

If You Made a Million 82–91

I'm in Charge of Celebrations 92–100

Alejandro's Gift 101–108

Rocking and Rolling 109–118

The Armadillo from Amarillo 119–127

Visitors from Space 128–135

Skills and Strategies Index 136

Printed in the United States of America

ISBN 0-15-312713-9

13 14 054 2007 2006 2005 2004

Name _____

► **Complete the sentences with words from the stars.**

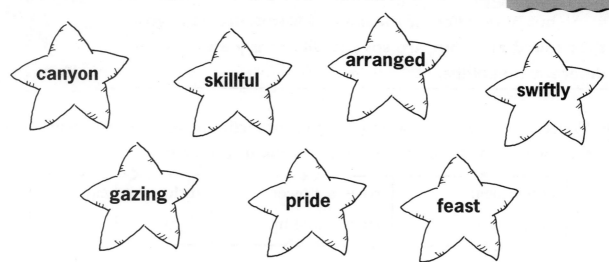

canyon

skillful

arranged

swiftly

gazing

pride

feast

1. We prepared a _____ at our campsite tonight.

2. Later, our _____ cook made a delicious dessert for us.

3. After dinner we all sat around _____ up at the stars.

4. Some stars seemed to be _____ in patterns.

5. After stargazing, we walked to the edge of the _____.

6. We looked down at the _____ moving river.

7. I took great _____ in having chosen such a beautiful place for our camping trip.

► **Write the words from the stars that match the definitions below.**

8. taking a long look at something _____

9. able to do something very well _____

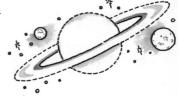

10. celebration with lots of food _____

SCHOOL-HOME CONNECTION With your child, discuss sights in nature that you both enjoy. Use at least three of the Vocabulary Words in your discussion.

Harcourt

Name _____

Skill Reminder **Homographs:** words that are spelled the same but have different meanings. **Homophones:** words that sound alike but are spelled differently and have different meanings.

▶ Write the correct meaning for the underlined word in each sentence. Choose from the pairs of homographs in the chart.

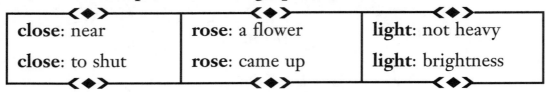

close: near	**rose**: a flower	**light**: not heavy
close: to shut	**rose**: came up	**light**: brightness

1. The sun is bright because it is so <u>close</u> to us. _____

2. We can see the <u>light</u> of the stars when it is dark. _____

3. When morning came, the sun <u>rose</u> in the sky. _____

▶ Write the correct word in each sentence. Choose from the pairs of homophones in the chart.

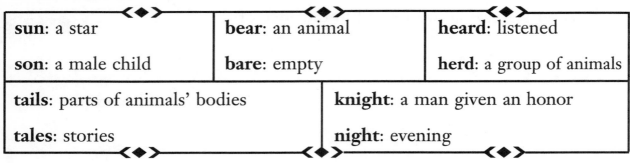

sun: a star	**bear**: an animal	**heard**: listened
son: a male child	**bare**: empty	**herd**: a group of animals
tails: parts of animals' bodies	**knight**: a man given an honor	
tales: stories	**night**: evening	

4. The _____ is the star closest to the earth.

5. People look at the _____ sky and see groups of stars.

6. People told stories, or _____, about the stars.

7. Other people _____ these stories.

8. Some stories were about animals, such as a great _____ or a fox.

Harcourt

Name _____

▶ Before you read "Coyote Places the Stars," fill in the first column of the chart below. Fill in the second column when you have finished reading the story. Remember to include only the main ideas.

☆ ☆ ☆ **Prediction Chart** ☆ ☆ ☆

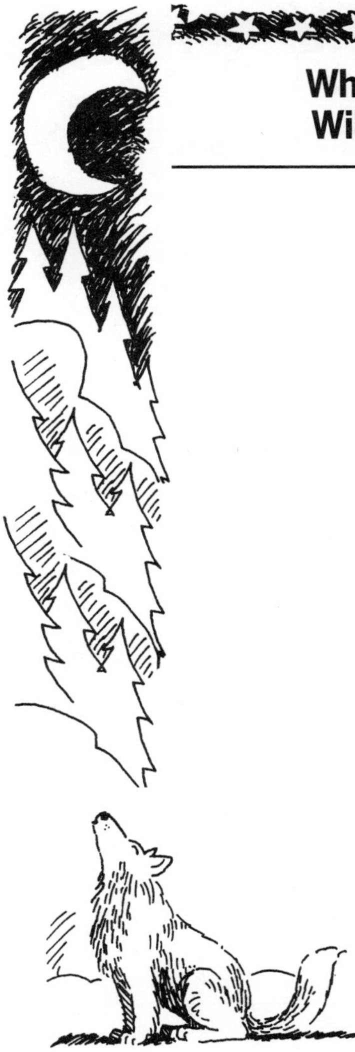

What I Think Will Happen	What Actually Happens

▶ Why do the other animals say that Coyote is the most clever and crafty of all animals?

_____

_____

_____

Journeys of Wonder **5**

Harcourt

Name _____

▶ **Write the sentences in the correct order to tell about what happens in "Coyote Places the Stars." The first one has been started for you.**

- Second, Coyote wonders if he can move the stars.
- After the animals come, they form a circle and look at the sky.
- Later, Coyote howls and all the animals come.
- Finally, the animals have a feast for Coyote.
- First, Coyote climbs an arrow ladder to the moon.
- Next, Coyote shoots arrows and places the stars in animal shapes.

1. First, _____

_____

2. _____

_____

3. _____

_____

4. _____

_____

5. _____

_____

6. _____

_____

Harcourt

Name _____

▶ **Read the passage and then answer the questions. Fill in the oval next to your choice.**

The animals were happy with the star shapes Coyote had created. They cheered for him and planned a feast. First, they gathered food from the desert. Then, they found a special treat to give to Coyote. Next, they found Coyote and began the celebration. Later that evening, after they had finished eating, they sang and danced. Finally, when everyone was tired from the great feast, they rested and looked forward to seeing the star shapes the next night.

1 What happened first?
- ⬭ The animals sang and danced.
- ⬭ The animals gathered food from the desert.
- ⬭ The animals looked forward to the next night.
- ⬭ The animals rested.

2 Then what happened?
- ⬭ The animals looked at their star shapes.
- ⬭ The animals planned a feast.
- ⬭ The animals cheered for Coyote.
- ⬭ The animals found something special for Coyote.

3 What happened next?
- ⬭ The animals found Coyote and celebrated.
- ⬭ The animals helped Coyote.
- ⬭ The animals gave Coyote a special treat.
- ⬭ The animals gathered food.

4 What happened after they ate?
- ⬭ They rested.
- ⬭ They sang and danced.
- ⬭ They gave Coyote a treat.
- ⬭ They thanked Coyote.

5 What happened last?
- ⬭ The animals danced.
- ⬭ The animals found food.
- ⬭ The animals looked at the star shapes.
- ⬭ The animals rested.

Harcourt

Name _____

► **Choose the correct word from each pair in parentheses ( ) to complete the sentence. Write the word on the line.**

1. Coyote decided to _____ his arrows into the sky.

(shoot, chute)

2. The arrows shot _____ the sky and toward the moon.

(through, threw)

3. Coyote stayed away for several _____.

(daze, days)

4. The _____ sky looks different in Australia than it does in North America. **(knight, night)**

5. One of the star groups is named after a big _____.

(bear, bare)

6. To see the stars really well, go down the

_____, away from the lights.

(road, rode)

7. The full moon _____ at about 9:00 P.M.

(rows, rose)

8. Can you _____ the North Star?

(sea, see)

9. Coyote stood _____ and explained what he had done.

(there, their)

10. The animals thought Coyote had done _____ work.

(great, grate)

 TRY THIS! Choose a few pages in a book. See how many words you can find that have homophones. Use three of them in sentences of your own.

Harcourt

Name _____

▶ **Circle the adjective in each sentence. Underline the noun it describes.**

1. Graceful deer moved across the desert.

2. The lizards were slow.

3. Silvery fish splashed up the stream.

4. A great eagle soared in the sky.

5. Coyote was glad.

▶ **Think of an adjective to describe each underlined noun. Rewrite the sentence, adding the adjective.**

6. Coyote was an <u>artist</u>.

   _____

7. He made a <u>ladder</u> to the moon.

   _____

8. He moved the stars with <u>arrows</u>.

   _____

9. Now the stars make <u>pictures</u>.

   _____

10. The pictures light the <u>sky</u>.

    _____

 TRY THIS! Think of a scene you might see from your window at night. Write five sentences to describe it. Circle the adjectives you used.

Harcourt

Name _____

▶ **Write the Spelling Word from the box that best
completes each sentence.**

storm	horse	morning	forest

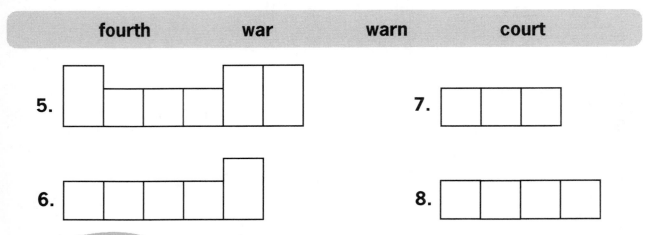

I like to ride my **(1)** _____. One

(2) _____ we left at dawn.

We rode into the **(3)** _____. When it

looked as if a **(4)** _____ was coming,
we went back home.

▶ **Write the Spelling Word that fits each shape.**

fourth	war	warn	court

5. ▯

6. ▯

7. ▯

8. ▯

Handwriting Tip: When you join *o* to another letter, be sure that it
doesn't look like an *a*. Write these words.

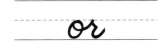

9. form _____   **10.** porch _____

SCHOOL-HOME CONNECTION Talk with your child about events of the day,
both in your family and in the news. List words with the /ôr/ sound that you
hear in *warm*, *important*, and *tortillas*, and read them aloud with your child.

Harcourt

Name _____

▶ **Complete each animal's sentence or sentences with a word from the box.**

nonsense	grumbling	mischief	
duty	council	summons	satisfied

1. I wonder what this _____ meeting is all about.

2. I don't know. I just got the _____ this morning.

3. Maybe I've been _____ about the heat too much lately.

4. Maybe it's because I've been causing _____ in the trees.

5. I feel it's my _____ to tell you that you've been staying up too late.

6. That's complete _____!

7. Quiet, everyone. Your curiosity is about to be _____.

▶ **Answer the following questions with words from the box above.**

8. If you cause a lot of trouble, what are you making? _____

9. If you are responsible for doing a job, what do you have?

a _____

10. If you are happy about someone or something, how do you feel? _____

TRY THIS! Imagine that animals can talk. Write a paragraph about a meeting of some pets. Use as many Vocabulary Words as you can.

Harcourt

Skill Reminder   Sequence is the order of events in a story. Words such as *first, next, then,* and *finally* are time-order words.

▶ Read the poem. Find the time-order word or words in each sentence and write them on the line.

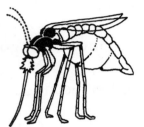

1. First, the mosquito so small
   Tells the iguana a tale so very tall.

1. _____

2. Next, iguana puts sticks in each ear,
   And python thinks he has a lot to fear.

2. _____

3. After looking for a safe place to hide,
   The python burrows by rabbit's side.

3. _____

4. Then, the rabbit runs away,
   While the crow tells all not to stay.

4. _____

5. When monkey hears the cry,
   He bounds through treetops so high.

5. _____

6. Next, a limb falls on a nest,
   Killing an owlet who is at rest.

6. _____

7. Mother Owl, then, will not wake the sun,
   Until the blame is placed and done.

7. _____

8. The story goes backward until, finally,
   The mosquito is hiding in a tree.

8. _____

Harcourt

Name _____

► As you read "Why Mosquitoes Buzz in People's Ears," look for what the characters say and do. Fill in the character chart below up until the time the animals gather at the council meeting.

Character	What the Character Says	What the Character Does
mosquito		
iguana		
snake		
rabbit		
crow		
monkey		
Mother Owl		
owlets		
King Lion		

► In what ways do the animal characters in this story act like people?

_____

_____

_____

TRY THIS! Write a conversation that you think two pets in a household might have. They can be your own pets, the pets of someone you know, or two pets you make up.

Harcourt

Name _____

▶ Write the words from the box in the correct columns below. Then divide each word into syllables. Examples have been done for you.

summons	nonsense	daytime	mammal	likely	treetop
sudden	hopeful	waterhole	nearby	uncertain	council

VCCV Pattern	Compound Words	Words with Prefixes or Suffixes
burrow bur-row	somehow some-how	disappoint dis-ap-point
1.	5.	9.
2.	6.	10.
3.	7.	11.
4.	8.	12.

TRY THIS! With a partner, think of more words that fit each category. Add them to the chart above.

Harcourt

Name _____

▶ **On the lines, write two words from the box for the sounds each animal makes.**

purr	caw	whinny	bark
tweet	woof	meow	neigh

1. _____   5. _____

2. _____   6. _____

3. _____   7. _____

4. _____   8. _____

Did you know that different languages use different words for animal sounds?

Yes. In America ducks say "quack, quack." In Mexico ducks say "cua, cua," and in China ducks say "ya-ya"!

EARTH

 TRY THIS! Write and illustrate a story about a group of animals. In your story, use animal sounds.

Harcourt

Name _____

Why Mosquitoes
Buzz in
People's Ears

Grammar:
Adjectives for
What Kind

▶ **Circle the adjective in each sentence. Underline the noun it describes.**

1. The rabbit was afraid.

2. The large snake could eat her.

3. The naughty mosquito started everything.

4. Her little joke hurt the owl.

5. She found herself in big trouble.

▶ **Think of an adjective to describe each underlined noun. The adjective should answer the question in parentheses ( ). Rewrite the sentence, adding the adjective.**

6. A <u>monkey</u> heard the crow. (What size?)

_____

7. He was eating a <u>mango</u>. (How does it taste?)

_____

8. The monkey climbed a <u>tree</u>. (What shape?)

_____

9. The <u>bark</u> scratched him. (How does it feel?)

_____

10. He stopped to chew a <u>leaf</u>. (What color?)

_____

 TRY THIS! Think of a zoo animal you like. Write sentences that tell how it looks, sounds, feels, and smells. Circle the adjectives you use.

Name _____

▶ **Write the Spelling Words from the box to complete
the sentences.**

| our | heard | weigh | herd | way | hour |

"Have you **(1)** _____ about the **(2)** _____ of
animals that trampled over our field last week?" asked Barry. "They ran all

the **(3)** _____ down to the river. Can you imagine

what all those animals must **(4)** _____?

In just about an **(5)** _____, they

changed the look of **(6)** _____ field."

▶ **Write a Spelling Word from the box to match each picture.**

| one | won | flower | flour |

7. _____

8. _____

9. _____

10. _____

Handwriting Tip: Loop an *e* so it doesn't look like an *i*.
Write these words.

_____

e

11. heard _____

12. weigh _____

SCHOOL-HOME CONNECTION With your child, make up
sentences that use pairs of homophones. Here are a few
examples: Add the prices in that *ad*. I'll be walking down the *aisle*.

Journeys of Wonder **17**

Harcourt

Name _____

► **Read the words on the books. Then write the word that answers each riddle.**

reteller

sprawled

success

career

editor

perfect

1. I am a person who helps writers make books.

   What am I? an _____

2. I am a word that means "to make something just right."

   What word am I? to _____

3. I am more than just a job. I am something for which you work

   very hard. What am I? a _____

4. I am a word that tells what you did when you lounged, stretched

   out, and relaxed. What word am I? _____

5. I am someone who puts stories into my own words.

   What am I? a _____

6. I am the opposite of *failure*. What am I? _____

► **Write the Vocabulary Word that best completes each set of related words.**

7. rested, stretched, relaxed _____

8. improve, revise, fix _____

SCHOOL-HOME CONNECTION Play a game of Concentration with your child, using pairs of Vocabulary Words on index cards. Try to define the word when you find a match.

Harcourt

Name _____

Skill Reminder   The order in which things happen is the sequence of events.

▶ **Read the paragraphs below. Then complete the chart with dates and events in Hans Christian Andersen's life.**

Hans Christian Andersen was born in 1805 and grew up in Denmark. Hans's father read his son stories such as *The Arabian Nights*. He also built Hans a puppet stage so that Hans could act out the stories he read.

In 1819, when Hans was just 14, he left home and went to work in the theater. In 1827 he went to school to learn more about acting. He wrote many plays during this time, but none of them became successful.

Finally, in 1835, his first book of stories was published. It was called *Tales Told for Children*, and included stories such as "The Princess and the Pea," "The Ugly Duckling," and "The Snow Queen." Then, in 1855, he published the story of his life, *Fairy Tale of My Life*. Hans Christian Andersen died in 1875.

Date	Event
1805	
	Hans Christian Andersen left home and went to work in the theater.
1827	
1835	
1855	
	Hans Christian Andersen died.

Harcourt

Name _____

▶ As you read "A Bookworm Who Hatched,"
complete the sequence chart below. Write about
Verna Aardema's life and the events that led to her
career as a writer.

When	Event

▶ Why did the author run off to her *secret room*? How did it help in
her career?

_____

_____

_____

Harcourt

Name _____

▶ Read each sentence that has to do with "A Bookworm Who Hatched." Write *F* in front of the sentence if it is a fact. Write *O* in front of the sentence if it is an opinion.

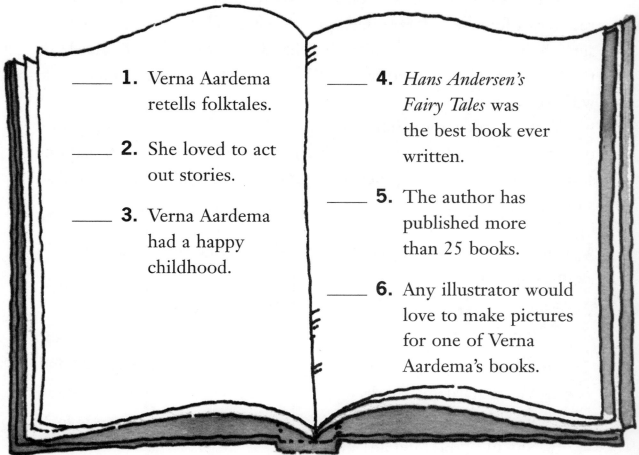

_____ **1.** Verna Aardema retells folktales.

_____ **2.** She loved to act out stories.

_____ **3.** Verna Aardema had a happy childhood.

_____ **4.** *Hans Andersen's Fairy Tales* was the best book ever written.

_____ **5.** The author has published more than 25 books.

_____ **6.** Any illustrator would love to make pictures for one of Verna Aardema's books.

▶ Write two sentences that tell facts you read in "A Bookworm Who Hatched." Then write two sentences that tell your opinion about the selection. Write *F* for fact or *O* for opinion after your sentences.

7. _____

8. _____

9. _____

10. _____

Harcourt

SCHOOL-HOME CONNECTION With your child, find and read an advertisement in a magazine or newspaper. Write two facts and two opinions found in the advertisement. Talk about the differences.

Name _____

▶ **Read the paragraphs and then answer the questions.
Fill in the oval next to your choice.**

Verna Aardema has written more than 25 books. She calls herself a reteller of folktales. Before deciding on what folktale to retell, she makes sure she likes the folktale and that it has a good story. Verna Aardema thinks that writing is hard but that its rewards are great. I don't think she will ever stop writing.

Verna Aardema was born on June 6, 1911. The first book she ever owned was *Hans Andersen's Fairy Tales*. As a child, she loved to act out stories as well as make up new ones. Now, as an adult, she is a fantastic storyteller.

1 Which of these is an opinion in the passage?

⬭ Verna Aardema is a fantastic storyteller.

⬭ She is a reteller of folktales.

⬭ Verna Aardema thinks writing is not easy.

⬭ She likes the folktales she retells.

2 Which of these is an opinion in the passage?

⬭ Verna Aardema was born on June 6, 1911.

⬭ *Hans Andersen's Fairy Tales* was the first book she owned.

⬭ Verna Aardema thinks the rewards of writing are great.

⬭ She will never stop writing.

3 Which describes a fact?

⬭ something that can be proven

⬭ something that a person thinks is pretty or good

⬭ what one person believes

⬭ what one person is feeling

4 Which describes an opinion?

⬭ something that can be proven

⬭ something that can be seen

⬭ a person's feelings

⬭ something that is true

Harcourt

Name _____

Title Page	Tells title, author, and publisher.
Copyright Page	Tells when the book was published.
Table of Contents	Lists units, chapters, lesson titles, and their starting pages.
Glossary	Lists key words, their pronunciations, and their meanings.
Index	Lists topics in alphabetical order with page numbers.

▶ **Suppose you are reading a book about famous authors. Read each question. Then write what part of the book you would look in to find the answer.**

1. What is the complete title of the book you are reading?

_____

2. What is the meaning of a word in the book? _____

3. On what page does Chapter 6 begin? _____

4. Who wrote the book? _____

5. On what pages is Hans Christian Andersen talked about?

_____

6. When was the book published? _____

7. Which chapter is called "Early Children's Authors," Chapter 3

or Chapter 4? _____

8. Who published the book? _____

SCHOOL-HOME CONNECTION With your child, look through some books. Identify the book parts and the information found in each one.

Harcourt

Name _____

▶ **Read the sentences below. Think about how the first
two underlined words go together. Then write a word
from the box to complete the analogy. A sample sentence is done
for you.**

kitten	sad	light	Dad	quiet	
dry	small	water	out	soft	see

Night is to day as dark is to **light**.

1. Huge is to large as tiny is to _____.

2. Loud is to noisy as silent is to _____.

3. Hot is to cold as hard is to _____.

4. New is to old as happy is to _____.

5. Rough is to smooth as wet is to _____.

6. Mother is to Mom as Father is to _____.

7. Up is to down as in is to _____.

8. Ski is to snow as swim is to _____.

9. Dog is to puppy as cat is to _____.

10. Nose is to smell as eye is to _____.

 TRY THIS! Write three analogies of your own for someone to figure out. Leave a blank in each sentence. Write the answers on the back of the page.

24 Journeys of Wonder

Name _____

▶ **Circle the adjective in each sentence. Underline the noun it describes.**

1. There were nine children in the family.

2. One photograph shows the children.

3. Evelyn was the oldest in the picture.

4. After that, no photographers came by.

5. Several children were left out.

▶ **Think of an adjective to describe each underlined noun. The adjective should tell how many. Rewrite the sentence, adding the adjective.**

6. Verna Aardema heard <u>stories</u> from Africa.

   _____

7. She filled <u>sheets</u> of paper with the tales.

   _____

8. She talked to <u>editors</u> in the city.

   _____

9. Writing a book can take <u>years</u>.

   _____

10. Verna Aardema has <u>readers</u> of all ages.

   _____

Harcourt

SCHOOL-HOME CONNECTION Have your child write sentences about the number of brothers and sisters he or she has. Use adjectives that tell how many. (Remember, *zero* tells how many, too!)

Name _____

▶ **Write a Spelling Word from the box to complete each sentence.**

| curl | burned | person | perfect | Thursday | skirt |

1. A _____ in my family turned five last week.

2. Her birthday was on _____.

3. Five candles _____ brightly on her cake.

4. One present was a beautiful red

   _____.

5. One guest wanted to _____ up on the couch.

6. The party was absolutely _____.

▶ **Write the Spelling Words from the box in alphabetical order.**

| thirty | birth | church | nurse |

7. _____   9. _____

8. _____   10. _____

Handwriting Tip: Close the letter *i* so it doesn't look like an *e*. Write these words.

11. thirty _____   12. skirt _____

SCHOOL-HOME CONNECTION Look over some ads or flyers that come in the mail. With your child, find and circle words with the /ûr/ sound you hear in *girl* and *fur*.

Harcourt

Name _____

▶ **Read the words on the cloud. Then read each pair of words on the dinner plates. Write the word from the cloud that goes best with each pair.**

uneventfully   varied   drizzle   portions

supplied

necessities   abandon   damaged

1. hurt
   harmed

   _____

2. changed
   differed

   _____

3. rain
   sprinkle

   _____

4. leave
   quit

   _____

5. servings
   amounts

   _____

6. gave
   provided

   _____

7. boringly
   unexcitingly

   _____

8. needs
   essentials

   _____

Harcourt

Name _____

Skill Reminder **Stories that are realistic tell about
things that could happen in real life. Stories that are
fantasies tell about things that are make-believe.**

▶ **Read the passage below. In the chart, list details that tell things
that could happen in real life and things that could only happen
in a fantasy story.**

It was a cloudy day. We were standing outside our house looking
at the sky. Suddenly food started to fall from the clouds. Bread, apples,
broccoli, and hamburgers landed on the ground. Our neighbors were eating
outside on their porch. Food was falling on them, but they didn't seem to
notice anything strange. They continued to eat as usual. The neighbors on
the other side of our house came outside to see what was happening. Then
they started to play catch with the food as it fell from the sky. Meanwhile
their dog and cat went inside the house to get some silverware for the food.

Real Life Details	Fantasy Details

 TRY THIS! Write a scene of your own. Include at least three realistic details and
at least three fantasy details.

Harcourt

Name _____

Skill Reminder   A fact is a statement that can be checked or proven. An opinion tells what someone thinks or feels.

▶ Read each statement. Write *fact* or *opinion*.

Adding is more fun than sleeping upside down.

My box of cereal is in the shape of a square.

1. _____

5. _____

A foot is longer than an inch.

Eight quarters equals two dollars.

2. _____

6. _____

1, 3, 5, 7, and 9 are odd numbers. 2, 4, 6, 8, and 10 are even numbers.

My broccoli tastes the best.

3. _____

7. _____

I can eat more bananas than anyone.

Multiplying is easy.

4. _____

8. _____

Harcourt

Name _____

▶ Before you read "Cloudy With a Chance of Meatballs," fill in your predictions in the first column. After you read the story, fill in the second column.

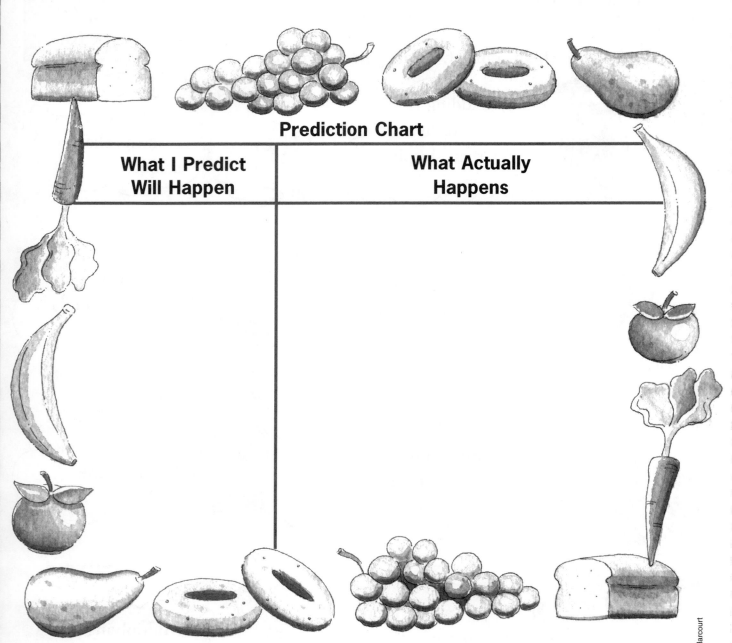

Prediction Chart

What I Predict Will Happen	What Actually Happens

▶ Why do you think the author wrote this story?

_____

_____

Harcourt

Name _____

▶ **Underline the figurative language in each of the sentences. Then rewrite each sentence to show what it really means.**

1. The yard was so full that the people felt as if they were in a suitcase.

_____

_____

2. The town became a garbage dump.

_____

3. After eating so much, everyone was feeling under the weather.

_____

_____

4. When I saw the food fall from the sky, my heart beat like a drum.

_____

_____

5. I felt happy from head to toe.

_____

6. The mayor lost control and was mad as a wet hen.

_____

7. My brother and I are like two peas in a pod.

_____

8. The people left their town as quick as a wink.

_____

Harcourt

Name _____

▶ **Complete each sentence using figurative language.**

1. The food fell from the sky as fast as

_____.

2. The food landed on her head so hard that she saw

_____.

3. The town became as messy as a

_____.

4. The people made their decision to leave town

just in the _____.

5. One man, who was as strong as

_____

single-handedly moved the town.

▶ **Write sentences using each of the phrases listed below. Use figurative language in your sentences.**

6. as hungry as

_____

7. as wild as

_____

8. as sweet as

_____

SCHOOL-HOME CONNECTION With your child, read a newspaper or magazine article. Look for figurative language in the article. Discuss the real meaning of each example you find.

Harcourt

Name _____

Cloudy With a
Chance of
Meatballs

Reading
Everyday
Sources

▶ **Write the reading source where you might find the information in each sentence below. You may use a source more than once.**

| newspaper | school newsletter | sign |
| advertisement | list | menu |

1. This way to dessert.

   _____

2. Remember to clean your plate.

   _____

3. headline: It Pours Meatballs!

   _____

4. Your choice of broccoli, spinach, carrots, or squash.

   _____

5. Reward for anyone who helps clean up our town.

   _____

6. School is cancelled due to too much food!

   _____

7. weather: Salt and Pepper Winds Hit ChewandSwallow

   _____

8. SALE Hamburgers at Dirt Cheap Prices

   _____

 TRY THIS! Write about two of the most recent everyday reading sources you looked at and why.

Harcourt

Name _____

▶ **For each weather word in the list, choose from the box two words that could relate to it. Write the milder word first and then the stronger word. Do not write any word more than once.**

gale	freezing	roar	rain	hot	storm
puffy	chilly	hurricane	blizzard	warm	
drizzle	rumble	flakes	pour	tornado	

	mild word	**strong word**
Example weather	warm	hot
1. snow	_____	_____
2. storm	_____	_____
3. wind	_____	_____
4. rain	_____	_____
5. temperature	_____	_____
6. clouds	_____	_____
7. climate	_____	_____
8. thunder	_____	_____

TRY THIS! Write a letter to a friend. Tell about your day in school, using six describing words. Then rewrite the letter, using stronger describing words.

Harcourt

Name _____

▶ **Circle the article in each sentence. Underline the noun it introduces.**

1. An orange fell on my head.

2. The rainstorm was very odd.

3. I worried about the weather.

4. A tornado made of spaghetti could be bad.

5. Who ever heard of a snowstorm of potatoes?

▶ **Complete each sentence, filling in the blank with *a* or *an*.**

6. Not _____ cloud filled the sky.

7. Then I heard _____ earthquake.

8. It was _____ terrible sound.

9. _____ meatball hit the ground.

10. It nearly hit _____ arcade.

11. I saw _____ child running.

12. Then _____ ambulance rushed by.

 TRY THIS! Make a list of five of your favorite foods. Decide whether to use *a*, *an,* or *the* before each word on your list. Then use each phrase in a sentence.

Harcourt

Name _____

▶ **Write the Spelling Words from the box that best complete the sentences.**

common	matter	supper	silly

Dear Aunt Betty,

That **(1)** _____ story you told about your new kitten

was funny. What could have been the **(2)** _____ with her?

Is it **(3)** _____ for a kitten to pick a fight with a dog? I had

better go now. Mom said **(4)** _____ is ready.

Your niece,
Mandy

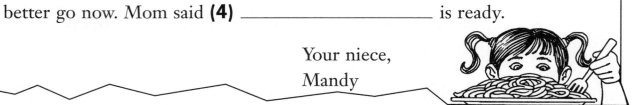

▶ **The underlined words are mixed up. Write the correct Spelling Word from the words in the box.**

butter	sudden	correct	collect

5. Is this the <u>rocterc</u> way to mash potatoes? _____

6. The <u>dusned</u> rainstorm surprised us. _____

7. Dwayne likes to <u>loctcel</u> stamps. _____

8. I like <u>tubtre</u> on my corn. _____

Handwriting Tip: Do not put letters too close together when
you write, or they will be hard to read. Write these words.

9. lesson _____ **10.** letter _____

SCHOOL-HOME CONNECTION With your child, make a list of words that
have double consonants, like *ribbon*, *ladder*, *ruffle*, and *button*. Then make
up silly sentences using pairs of those words chosen at random.

Harcourt

Name _____

▶ **Complete each sentence with a word from the box.**

wits	wailing	advice	dreadful	faring	farewell

1. Follow these words of

_____ on giving a

great outdoor party.

2. First, remember to keep your

_____ about you.

Don't get nervous.

3. It would be _____ if your guests felt too crowded, so have your party in a park.

4. Don't play the music too loudly, or the dogs in the park might

start _____.

5. Check on your guests from time to time to see how they

are _____. If the party seems slow, play a game.

6. If everything goes well, your guests will be smiling as they

say _____.

▶ **Answer each riddle with the correct word from the box above.**

7. I am what guests say when they are leaving.

What word am I? _____

8. I am helpful information a person gives you.

What word am I? _____

Harcourt

Name _____

Skill Reminder   A fact can be proved. An opinion is someone's belief.

▶ **Read the advertisements below. Decide which statements are facts and which ones are opinions. Then answer the questions.**

1. What are the facts in this advertisement?

_____

_____

_____

2. What are the opinions in this advertisement?

_____

_____

_____

3. What are the facts in this advertisement?

_____

_____

_____

4. What are the opinions in this advertisement?

_____

_____

_____

Best Sale in History!

There's no better place to get the car of your dreams.
We've got the latest models.

Cars Unlimited

89 Colonial Rd.
Mon.–Sun. 8–8

Is your current home too crowded?
Are you stuck without a yard?
Come and see our great, new model homes. You won't believe the space. Two-, three-, and four-bedroom homes.
Gorgeous landscaping and 2-car garage.
Pool and other options Available.

Interior Builders

Harcourt

Name _____

▶ Complete the story map below as you read "The Crowded House." List only the most important events.

Story Map

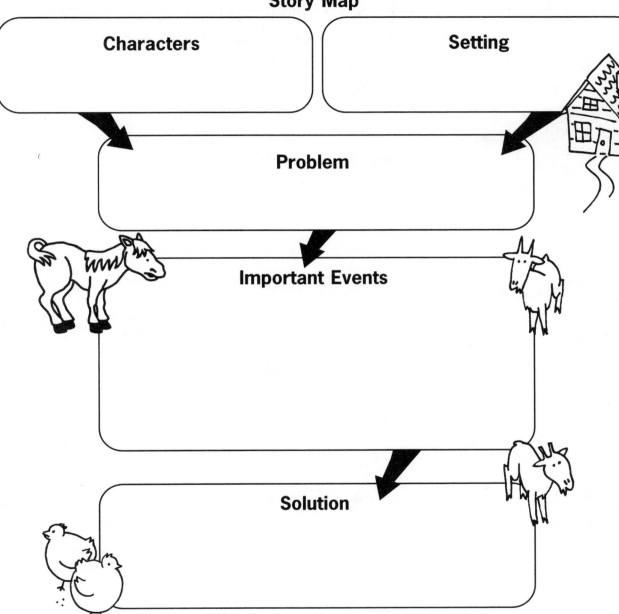

Characters

Setting

Problem

Important Events

Solution

▶ Do you think Bartholomew gave good advice? Explain.

_____

_____

_____

Harcourt

Name _____

▶ **Read the paragraph and the advertisement. Answer the questions.**

Can you imagine how crowded it would be for eleven people and farm animals to live in one room? You would feel very uncomfortable. Where would you keep your clothes and toys? There wouldn't be much room to play or to eat. Sleeping would probably be hard, too. In a one-room house, you might never have a spot that is really your own.

1. Skim the paragraph. What is the topic? _____

2. Scan the paragraph for four key words or ideas about the topic. List

them. _____

_____

Visit Uncle Tim's Farm

- see more than 50 animals
- ride a pony
- feed chickens
- take a hayride
- milk a goat or cow

Admission $8.00 for adults, $5.00 for children

Open Tuesday–Sunday 10–6

State Road 40 just west of Samson City

3. Skim this ad. What is being advertised? _____

4. Scan the ad for four key words or ideas about what is being advertised.

List them. _____

_____

 TRY THIS! Look through an article in a magazine or a newspaper. Skim the article for the topic. Scan it for words or ideas that tell about the topic. Write whether you would want to read the article and why.

Harcourt

Name _____

▶ **Read the paragraph. Look for clues to what the underlined words mean. Then write each word next to its definition.**

Last Sunday, Father got the horse and <u>buggy</u>, and we all rode to Aunt Lydia's in the country. Mother wore her best <u>bonnet</u> to keep her hair from blowing. She had on her good <u>petticoat</u>, which makes her overskirt stand out like an umbrella. Mother and Aunt Lydia did not run and play, of course. They sat and wrote letters with a <u>quill pen</u>. We boys started to play <u>hoops</u>, but Father said we must not get dirty until the photographer had made a <u>tintype</u> of the family. The little girls never get messy. They just sew on their <u>samplers</u>. This whole afternoon was a nice change from the everyday chores at home, like <u>churning</u> butter.

1. writing tool made from a feather _____

2. vehicle pulled by a horse _____

3. a very full slip worn under a skirt _____

4. kind of hat _____

5. game with round objects _____

6. something to practice stitches on _____

7. mixing to make a food _____

8. old kind of photograph _____

TRY THIS! List some words you use today that you think will not be used in 200 years. Tell why you think so.

Harcourt

Name _____

▶ **Read the choices of adjectives in parentheses ( ) in
each sentence. Then underline the correct one.**

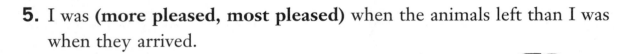

1. Is a donkey **(quicker, quickest)** than a goat?

2. That is the **(stronger, strongest)** donkey I've
   ever seen.

3. Chickens are the **(more colorful, most colorful)**
   of all the birds in the pen.

4. I am **(fonder, fondest)** of my children than of my animals.

5. I was **(more pleased, most pleased)** when the animals left than I was
   when they arrived.

▶ **Rewrite each sentence, using the correct
form of the adjective in parentheses ( ).**

6. The goat was **(swift)** than a deer.

   _____

7. The house was **(crowded)** than I expected.

   _____

8. Bartholomew was the **(smart)** man I knew.

   _____

9. The **(small)** of the eight children was in bed.

   _____

10. Molly was the **(skillful)** of all the children.

   _____

 TRY THIS! Make a picture book drawing to show tall, taller, and tallest.
Then use each word in a sentence of your own.

Harcourt

Name _____

▶ **Write a Spelling Word from the box to complete each sentence.**

| bigger | cooler | wisest | faster | slowest | louder |

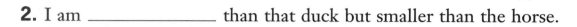

1. I can run _____ than anyone here.

2. I am _____ than that duck but smaller than the horse.

3. I am the _____ runner here.

4. This pond feels much _____ than the lake.

5. When I crow, I am _____ than any of those hens.

6. I am the _____ one in this smart crowd.

▶ **Write the Spelling Word that goes with each definition.**

| hottest | shorter | soonest | kindest |

7. most heated _____   **9.** less tall _____

8. most quickly _____   **10.** most thoughtful _____

Handwriting Tip: Be sure your letters all slant in the same direction. Write these words.

cooler

11. wisest _____   **12.** shorter _____

SCHOOL-HOME CONNECTION With your child, look around your home for items that can be compared, and then make up sentences comparing them. Here is an example: *The couch is bigger than the chair.*

Journeys of Wonder   **43**

Harcourt

Name _____

▶ **Choose from the words in the box. Write the Vocabulary Word that matches each definition.**

glistened	county	galloped	clutched	bid	auctioneer

1. held tightly   _____

2. shined, sparkled   _____

3. part of a state   _____

4. offer to buy   _____

5. leader of an auction _____

6. ran fast, like a horse _____

▶ **Complete the story below with words from the box.**

Stacey **(7)** _____ the reins on the horse

as it **(8)** _____ along. She had bought the

beautiful horse at the **(9)** _____ fair.

She had offered the highest **(10)** _____ for it.
With enough practice, Stacey would become a good rider.

 TRY THIS!   Write your own story about a pony. Use at least two of the Vocabulary Words in your story.

Harcourt

Name _____

Skill Reminder Every syllable has at least one vowel.
Use familiar patterns of vowels and consonants to help
you read longer words that look new.

▶ Fill in the chart. Divide each word in the chart into syllables. An
example is done for you.

Word	Number of Syllables	1st Syllable	2nd Syllable	3rd Syllable
satin	2	sat	in	
1. husky				
2. coffee				
3. borrowed				
4. tractor				
5. grasshoppers				
6. fertilize				
7. grocery				
8. auctioneer				

TRY THIS! Look in textbooks to find words that can be divided into two or more
syllables. Make a chart similar to the one above. Then use a dictionary
to check your pronunciations.

Harcourt

Skill Reminder Some everyday reading sources are newspapers, school newsletters, lists, menus, and advertisements. Each source gives different information.

street signs	newspaper	traffic signs
map	list	

▶ Suppose Leah's family is having a sale of their own. Use a reading source from the box to complete each sentence. You may use a source more than once.

Leah's father puts an ad in the **(1)** _____ to

inform people about the sale. He includes a **(2)** _____ with directions so people can find the farm. He also includes a

(3) _____ of the farm equipment he wants to sell.

When driving through town, there are many **(4)** _____ to obey. As people arrive near the farm, they read many

(5) _____ until they find the one that leads to Leah's house.

Some people take the highway home. There are **(6)** _____ on the highway to help travelers be safe. Leah's father helps people with

directions home by making a **(7)** _____.

After everyone leaves, he looks at his

(8) _____ to see if everything was sold.

Harcourt

Name _____

▶ Complete this story map as you read "Leah's Pony." List only the most important events.

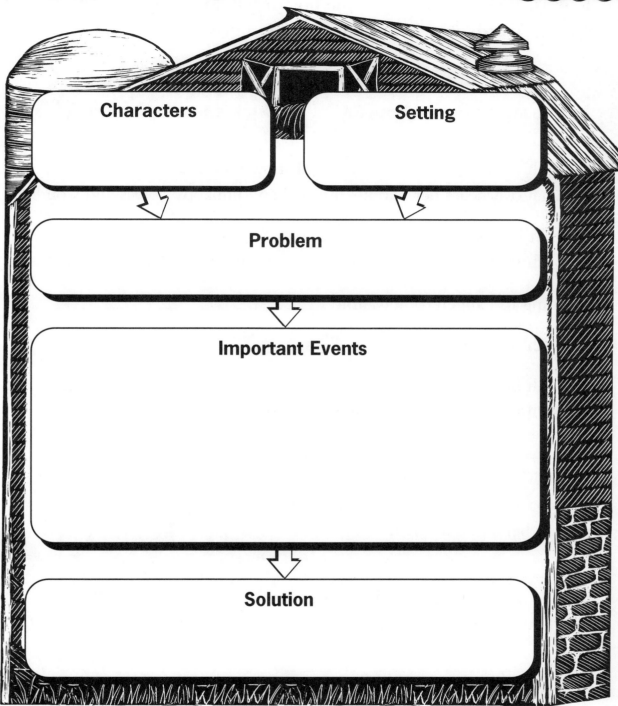

Characters

Setting

Problem

Important Events

Solution

▶ Why do you think Leah gives up the pony she loves?

_____

_____

Harcourt

Name _____

▶ **Read each of the following sentences about Leah's actions. Write a word from the box to tell how she is feeling. Words may be used more than once.**

happy	worried	sad	brave
unselfish	hopeful	frightened	proud

1. Leah loves to brush her pony and show him off. _____

2. Leah overhears her parents' hushed and unhappy voices and wonders

   what is going on. _____

3. Leah rides her pony so that she doesn't have to think about what is

   going to happen to her family. _____

4. Leah sells her pony. _____

5. Leah bids one dollar for the tractor. _____

6. Leah walks up and hands her dollar to the auctioneer.

   _____

7. After the auction, Leah smiles as Papa and Mama get back everything that belonged to them.

   _____

8. The next morning, Leah hears a whinny and runs to hug her pony.

   _____

TRY THIS! Think of a television or cartoon character. Picutre something that character likes to do. Describe how the character feels and what he or she does that shows that feeling.

Harcourt

Name _____

▶ **Read the passage and then answer the questions. Fill in the circle next to your choice.**

After the auction, Leah knew her family had a second chance to save the farm. She hugged her parents and told them that together they could make the farm a success. Leah smiled as she began making a list of all the things she could do on the farm. Then she and her pony visited neighbors and asked what they could trade for supplies. Leah was so busy that she had no time to worry that the farm wouldn't be a success. In fact, she even asked for a small piece of land to start her own vegetable garden. "I'm proud of you, Leah," said her father. "We couldn't keep the farm going without your help."

1 Leah is hopeful. What does she say to show how she feels?

- ⬤ She says that she wants to leave the farm.
- ⬤ She says she will help out.
- ⬤ She tells her parents that together they can make the farm a success.
- ⬤ She tells her parents that she wants to ride her pony.

2 Leah is determined. What action shows this?

- ⬤ She hugs her parents.
- ⬤ She makes a list of things she could do.
- ⬤ She rides her pony into town.
- ⬤ She works with her father.

3 Leah isn't worried that the farm won't be a success. Why?

- ⬤ She is proud of her family.
- ⬤ She never stops to ride her pony any more.
- ⬤ She begins a vegetable garden.
- ⬤ She is too busy to worry.

4 What does Leah's father say about Leah?

- ⬤ She is proud of him.
- ⬤ She is helpful.
- ⬤ She is keeping the farm going all by herself.
- ⬤ She can have some land for a vegetable garden.

Harcourt

Name _____

▶ **Read each sentence. Replace the underlined verb or phrase with a more vivid verb. You can use one of the verbs below or choose a different verb. Write the new sentence on the line.**

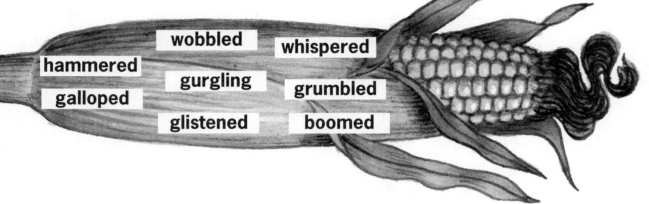

wobbled   whispered
hammered
gurgling   grumbled
galloped
glistened   boomed

1. Leah and her pony <u>ran</u> across the fields every day.

_____

2. She liked to brush the pony's coat until it <u>was clean</u>.

_____

3. She <u>said softly</u> in her pony's ear, "I am so glad I have you!"

_____

4. Leah liked to listen to the river <u>going</u> by.

_____

5. "I don't know how we can keep this farm," her father <u>said</u>.

_____

6. A man from the bank <u>put</u> a sign into the ground.

_____

7. Carrying heavy things, the neighbors <u>came</u> down the stairs.

_____

8. "Sold for one dollar!" the speaker <u>said</u> loudly.

_____

Harcourt

Name _____

▶ **Circle the action verb in each sentence.**

1. Leah rode her pony to the store.

2. The little pony kicked a stone.

3. The storekeeper admired the pony.

4. He bought the pony from Leah.

5. Later, he returned the pony to her.

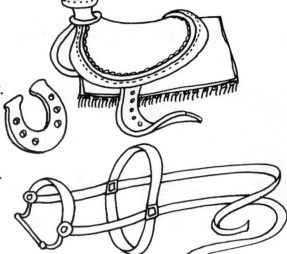

▶ **Choose a verb from the box to
complete the sentence. Then
write the sentence.**

stopped	sweeps	offered	stared	galloped

6. Leah _____ away on her pony.

_____

7. She _____ in front of Mr. B.'s store.

_____

8. Mr. B. _____ his front steps every day.

_____

9. Leah _____ to sell her pony to Mr. B.

_____

10. Mr. B. _____ at Leah in surprise.

_____

TRY THIS! Think of three interesting verbs that you could use in place of the verb *walked*. Write three sentences using your new verbs.

Harcourt

Name _____

▶ **Write a Spelling Word from the box to complete each sentence.**

| doorway | upstairs | sunset | downstairs |

When I go **(1)** _____, I open the

door. I watch the **(2)** _____ through the

hall **(3)** _____ before it gets dark. Then,

I go back **(4)** _____.

▶ **Write the Spelling Word that best completes each sentence.**

| outdoors | sunshine | bookcase | baseball |

5. The snow looks bright in the _____.

6. My favorite sport is

_____.

7. I like to camp _____.

8. She put two new books in the _____.

Handwriting Tip: Be sure to join all the letters in one word when you write it. Write these words.

_____

9. notebook _____   **10.** football _____

SCHOOL-HOME CONNECTION With your child, write each word on an index card: *after, noon, drive, way, life, guard, pop, corn*. Mix them up and place them face down. Take turns trying to pick pairs of cards that make compound words.

Harcourt

Name _____

▶ **Complete each sentence with a word from the box.**

cousins	fortunes	tumbleweeds
invisible	suspicious	budge

1. The three

_____ had
been close since childhood.

2. In times of trouble,

they would not _____
from each other's sides.

3. They trusted each
other and were never

_____.

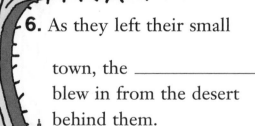

4. The _____
tie that held them
together was love.

5. One day, they decided
to go off to seek their

_____.

6. As they left their small

town, the _____
blew in from the desert
behind them.

▶ **Write the Vocabulary Word that best completes each set of related phrases below.**

7. not seen, out of sight, _____

8. move slightly, push aside, _____

SCHOOL-HOME CONNECTION With your child, take
turns choosing a word and naming other words that are
associated with it.

Journeys of Wonder **53**

Harcourt

Name _____

The Three Little
Javelinas

Characters'
Feelings and
Actions

Social Studies

Skill Reminder   You learn about a character through the words and actions of that character, the words of other characters, or an author's description.

▶ **Read the paragraph. Then fill in the web.**

The Navajo grandmother was named Kina. She had been the oldest member of her tribe for many years. Kina was an inspiration to the entire tribe because she was a great teacher. She patiently passed on the traditions of the tribe. Everyone loved to hear her stories. Kina always felt the respect and honor of the tribe.

Character

What She Is Like

What She Does

What She Feels

Harcourt

Name _____

Skill Reminder Authors use figurative language to help you form pictures in your mind.

▶ **Write the meaning of the underlined words in each sentence.**

1. The javelinas left a place that was <u>like an oven at 350 degrees</u>.

_____

2. A coyote ran through the desert <u>as fast as lightning</u>.

_____

_____

3. Coyote thought the pigs would be <u>as juicy as a watermelon</u>.

_____

4. Coyote was <u>as sneaky as a cat stalking a bird</u>.

_____

5. The saguaro was not <u>as pretty as a peacock</u>.

_____

6. Coyote showed his teeth, which were <u>as big as nails</u>.

_____

7. The third javelina built a house that was <u>as solid as an oak tree</u>.

_____

8. Coyote pretended to be <u>as weak as a kitten</u>.

_____

9. Coyote made himself <u>as skinny as a beanpole</u>.

_____

10. The javelinas were <u>as happy as larks in the springtime</u>.

_____

 Write three sentences of your own in which you use figurative language to describe three of your daily activities.

Name _____

▶ Complete the story map as you read "The Three
Little Javelinas." List only the most important events.

Story Map

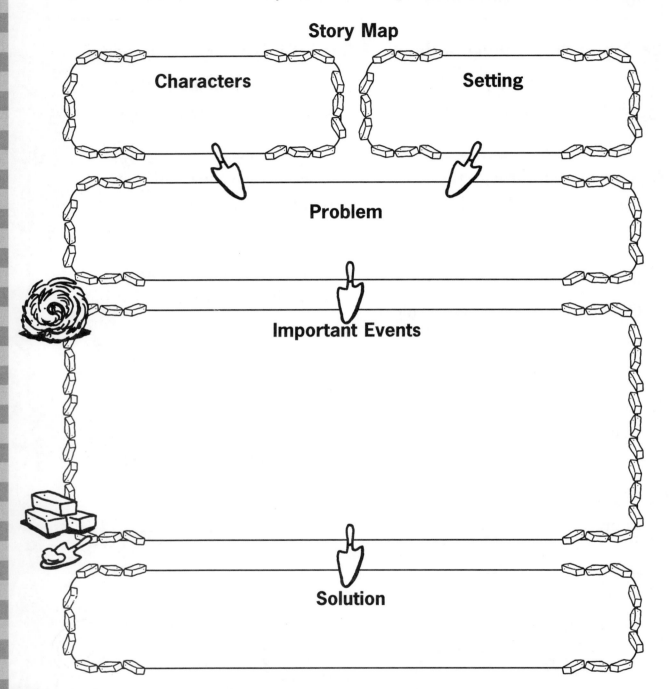

Characters

Setting

Problem

Important Events

Solution

▶ Why was the coyote able to blow down the first two houses and not
the third?

_____

_____

Harcourt

Name _____

▶ **Compare and contrast the two stories below. As you read, look for things that are alike and things that are different in each story.**

The Vegetable Garden

Once upon a time, in a faraway land, there lived a mother, a father, and their two children. They grew their own food in a vegetable garden near their little hut. One year it had been colder than usual, and the crops in their vegetable garden did not grow.

The boy had an idea. "Let us cover the crops with plastic," he said. "At night, it will keep the heat in and protect the plants from the cold."

The girl had an idea, too. "We should use clear plastic. That way, the sun can get through to the plants. We should also poke little holes in the plastic," she said. "That way, the plants won't get too hot." That year, the family had so many vegetables that they were able to sell some to the neighbors. It turned out to be a good year after all.

Too Much Fruit!

Once upon a time, in a tropical land where it was always warm, there lived a happy family. Their home was surrounded by fruit trees. They traded their fruit for different foods every Saturday. They would just carry baskets of fruit to the open-air market in town. There, they would choose vegetables, grains, and nuts offered by other families.

One year, they had so much fruit that it was rotting on the trees before they could trade it. "What a waste of good fruit," said the daughter. "We should do something to save it."

"I have an idea," said the son. "We can preserve the extra fruit by drying it. Then it will keep for a long time. We'll be able to trade with it all year."

GO ON ➡

Name _____

▶ Use the stories on page 57 to complete the diagram below. Below each story's title, list details that show how they are different. Then list four details that show how both stories are the same.

Both

7. _____

"The Vegetable Garden"

1. _____

_____

2. _____

8. _____

_____

3. _____

9. _____

10. _____

"Too Much Fruit!"

4. _____

5. _____

6. _____

 TRY THIS! Think about two games that are similar in some way, such as ball games, board games, or video games. Write the rules for each game, and then underline the parts that are similar.

Harcourt

Name _____

▶ **Write the word from the box that answers each riddle.**

javelina	cactus	chile	whirlwind	tumbleweed
coyote	saguaro	adobe	pueblo	dust storm

1. I am spicy.
I am used in sauces.

What am I? _____

2. I have many types.
I am prickly.

What am I? _____

3. I am like a pig.
I am wild.

What am I? _____

4. I am a small wolf.
I live in North America.

What am I? _____

5. I am shaped like a funnel.
I am made of air.

What am I?

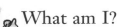
_____

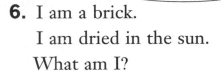

6. I am a brick.
I am dried in the sun.
What am I?

_____

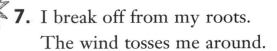

7. I break off from my roots.
The wind tosses me around.

What am I? _____

8. I am a desert plant.
I have armlike branches.

What am I? _____

9. I am like a village.
My buildings have flat roofs.

What am I? _____

10. I happen in dry areas.
I carry clouds of dust.

What am I? _____

TRY THIS! List two or three words that are special to the town or region where you live. You might choose names of foods, plants, or animals. Make up riddles for the words.

Harcourt

Name _____

▶ **Circle the helping verb in each sentence.**

    1. One javelina would collect tumbleweed.

    2. Another had used saguaro ribs for his house.

    3. Now the coyote has damaged both houses.

    4. The javelinas should rush to their sister's house.

    5. She had borrowed bricks from an adobe maker.

▶ **Complete each sentence with *have* or *has*.**

    6. The javelinas _____ shouted at the coyote.

    7. The coyote _____ arrived at the house.

    8. One javelina _____ peeked out the window.

    9. The coyote _____ puffed his best puff.

    10. The adobe bricks _____ not budged.

▶ **Complete each sentence with a helping verb and the correct form of the main verb in parentheses ( ).**

    11. The little javelinas _____ for joy. **(dance)**

    12. Their enemy _____ onto the roof. **(climb)**

 TRY THIS! Choose three verbs from this page that end with *-ed*. Use them to write your own sentences that include the helping verbs *have*, *has*, and *had*.

Name _____

▶ **Write Spelling Words from the box to complete the sentences.**

basket	always	until	Sunday	cactus	garden

Dad **(1)** _____ enjoys working in

the **(2)** _____. Every **(3)** _____

he checks to see how the **(4)** _____ he
planted is doing. The flowers won't be in bloom

(5) _____ July. Then, he will fill a

(6) _____ with flowers for the table.

▶ **On the line, write the Spelling Word that is spelled correctly.**

7. wellcome   welcome   _____

8. Monday   Moneday   _____

Handwriting Tip: Be sure an *n* does not look like an *m*. Write these words.

n

9. winter _____   **10.** invite _____

Harcourt

Name _____

▶ **Read each group of words listed below, and write the word that goes best with them. Choose from the words in the box.**

trading	schooner	harvest	
machete	pulp	bargain	support

1. soft part
meat

_____

2. help
hold up

_____

3. buying and selling
exchanging

_____

4. knife
ax

_____

5. ship
sailboat

_____

6. pick
gather

_____

7. make a deal
agree to buy

_____

▶ **Answer each riddle with a Vocabulary Word.**

8. I am a sharp tool used for cutting.

What am I? a _____

9. I am a large boat used for carrying goods to other places.

What am I? a _____

10. I am the soft, mushy part of a fruit or vegetable.

What am I? the _____

Harcourt

SCHOOL-HOME CONNECTION With your child, use some Vocabulary Words to discuss items in your home that come from other countries, such as clothing and food.

Name _____

Skill Reminder You can tell how a character feels by what the character says and does. Another clue is what other people in the story say about the character.

▶ Write the answer from the words and phrases in the box to best tell what the sentence says about the character.

| startled | careful | good workers | thirsty |
| worried | impatient | friendly | thoughtful |

1. Once the girl bit into a bitter cocoa bean before the chocolate was ready. This shows that the girl is _____.

2. They open coconuts and drink the sweet milk. This shows that they are _____.

3. When a hermit crab reaches for the girl, she squeals. This shows that she is _____.

4. When the sailor named Jacob sees the girl, he says hello with a big smile. This shows that he is _____.

5. The girl slowly puts the new bolt of cloth into a dry basket. This shows that she is _____.

6. Papa looks out at the thin sheet of ice, afraid it will not hold. This shows that Papa is _____.

7. The men clean snow off the river so the ice can freeze. This shows that the men are _____.

8. Mama makes hot chocolate to warm up her daughter. This shows that Mama is _____.

Harcourt

Name _____

Skill Reminder **When you compare, you look for things that are the same. When you contrast, you look for things that are different.**

▶ **Look at the picture. In the chart, write the things that are alike and things that are different.**

Compare	Contrast

TRY THIS! Make up menus for two dinners. Make sure each meal is the same in that it has protein (meat, fish, or beans), carbohydrate (potatoes, rice, or bread), and a vegetable. Also, make sure each meal is different in your choices.

Harcourt

Name _____

► Complete the Venn diagram below. In the outside
circles, write how the two places are different.
Where the circles overlap, write what is the same
about both places.

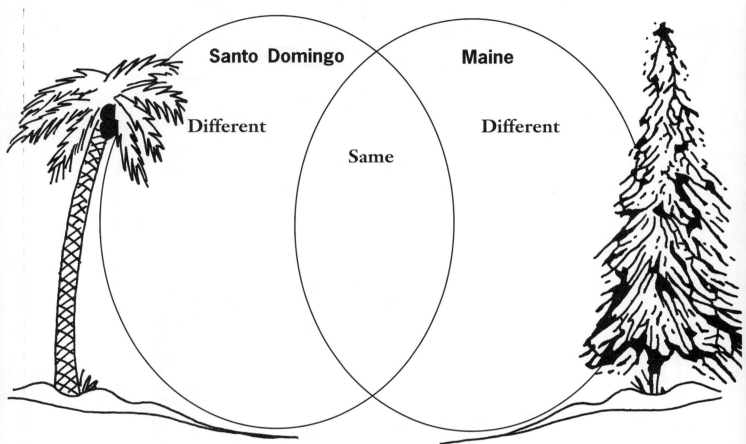

Santo Domingo   **Maine**

Different   Different

Same

► Why is the schooner as important to the people living in
Santo Domingo as to the people living in Maine?

_____

_____

_____

_____

_____

▶ **Suppose the letter below was written by the girl in Santo Domingo to the girl in Maine. Summarize what she says in the letter. Write your summary on the lines below.**

Dear Laura,

    You and I have never met, but your Uncle Jacob showed me pictures of you and where you live. I love looking at those pictures. They make me feel cold all over just like the ice that comes from where you live, Maine. It is always hot in Santo Domingo. Can you believe I've never seen snow or worn snow boots? It does rain here, though—a lot. I love my home, but someday I'd like to visit Maine. I hope you will write and tell me about your life.

        Your friend,

        Isabella

_____

_____

_____

_____

_____

Name _____

▶ **Read the paragraphs and then answer the questions.**
Fill in the oval next to your choice.

Do you like the taste of hot cocoa or a chocolate candy bar? Both of these products are made from cacao.

Cacao is a type of evergreen tree that grows in Central and South America. The tree has pink and yellow flowers and reddish fruits that grow on the tree's branches and trunk. It is the seed, or bean, inside the fruit of the cacao that is the source of cocoa, chocolate, and cocoa butter.

After the beans are harvested, they are dried and packed in bags for shipping. Cocoa beans are shipped to many parts of the world. Today, chocolate is popular almost everywhere.

1 The best summary for the first paragraph is

　⬭ People like drinking hot cocoa.

　⬭ Chocolate tastes good.

　⬭ Hot cocoa and chocolate are made from cacao.

　⬭ Cacao is a product.

2 The best summary for the second paragraph is

　⬭ The cacao bean is the source of cocoa, chocolate, and cocoa butter.

　⬭ Cacao grows in Central and South America.

　⬭ Cacao trees have pink flowers.

　⬭ Cacao is an evergreen tree.

3 The best summary for the third paragraph is

　⬭ Chocolate is made from cacao beans.

　⬭ Cacao beans and chocolate are shipped in bags.

　⬭ Cacao beans are dried before they are shipped.

　⬭ Cocoa beans are shipped almost everywhere.

4 When you write a summary, you should

　⬭ Copy sentences.

　⬭ Rewrite the paragraph in your own words.

　⬭ Tell the most important ideas in your own words.

　⬭ Tell all the details.

Harcourt

Name _____

▶ **Look at the maps of Maine and the Dominican Republic. Use them to answer these questions.**

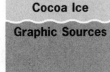

1. What is the capital of Maine?

_____

2. What is the capital of the Dominican Republic?

_____

3. Find the compass rose on the map. What do the letters on the compass rose stand for?

_____

_____

4. How would you describe the location of Santo Domingo?

_____

_____

5. Why do you think Santo Domingo is a major seaport of the Dominican Republic?

_____

_____

6. What body of water forms a border of Maine?

_____

7. What body of water forms the northern border of the Dominican Republic?

_____

8. On the map of Maine, what city is farther south?

Harcourt

Name _____

▶ **Read the following sentences. Write which graphic source from the box would be most helpful to use in each situation.**

| diagram | time line | schedule | map | table |

1. Mike's family wants to visit relatives in San Antonio, Texas. The relatives want to know when to meet Mike's family at the airport.

_____

2. Jordan wants to organize and compare information on the number of ships leaving Santo Domingo for Maine and the number leaving Maine

for Santo Domingo. _____

3. Kyle wants to find the capital of the Dominican Republic and the

capital of Maine. _____

4. Jeanne is doing a report on the history of Santo Domingo. She wants to show important events that relate to Santo Domingo.

_____

5. Tim is helping his brother make a model ship. They can't tell how the

pieces fit. _____

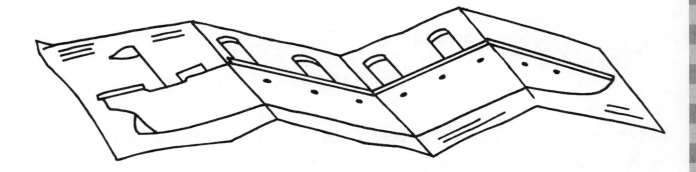

 TRY THIS! Find a graphic source shown in a science or social studies textbook. Explain to a partner the information it gives.

Harcourt

Name _____

▶ **Sort the words in the box into groups that go together. Write the words in the correct place.**

mango	mittens	schooner	banana	coat
rowboat	boots	orange	sailboat	hat

fruits

1. _____

2. _____

3. _____

clothes

4. _____

5. _____

6. _____

7. _____

boats

8. _____

9. _____

10. _____

TRY THIS! Imagine that you are shopping. You need school clothes, sports equipment, and writing supplies. Make lists of what you will buy. Give each list a different heading.

Harcourt

Name _____

▶ **Underline the verb. Label the subject *S* for singular or *P* for plural.**

1. Mama scoops pulp from a cacao pod.

2. She beats the pulp smooth and soft.

3. Cocoa ice tastes cold and sweet.

4. The slivers slide down my throat.

5. They keep me cool for hours.

▶ **Rewrite each sentence, using the correct present-tense form of the verb in parentheses ( ).**

6. Farmers _____ cocoa beans for ice. **(trade)**

   _____

7. Papa _____ a bolt of cloth. **(buy)**

   _____

8. One ship _____ ice and cloth. **(carry)**

   _____

9. He _____ it to me in the boat. **(pass)**

   _____

10. Our beans _____ to Maine. **(travel)**

   _____

Harcourt

Name _____

▶ **Write the Spelling Word from the box that best completes each sentence.**

belong	future	hotel	begin	music	pupil

What a trip! Our room in the **(1)** _____ is beautiful. We feel as if we **(2)** _____ here.

Tomorrow I will **(3)** _____ my hula lessons. I will be the youngest **(4)** _____ in the class. I just love the

(5) _____ that goes with hula dancing.

Maybe, in the **(6)** _____, I will be a famous hula dancer.

▶ **Write the Spelling Word that fits each shape.**

focus	cocoa	behind	tiger

7.

8.

9.

10.

Handwriting Tip: Be sure the letter *g* doesn't look like a *q*. Write these words. _____

g

11. tiger _____   **12.** begin _____

SCHOOL-HOME CONNECTION With your child, make up sentences using the Spelling Words and other words that have the vowel/consonant/vowel pattern. You might want to look through one of your child's textbooks for words.

Harcourt

Name _____

▶ **Write the word that matches each definition. Choose from the words in the box.**

rancher	profit	tending	corral	stray	market

1. in business, the money left over after paying bills _____

2. taking care of something _____

3. a place where many kinds of goods are bought and

   sold _____

4. a person whose job it is to raise large herds of

   animals _____

5. wander off, get lost _____

6. a pen or fenced area for animals _____

▶ **Complete each sentence with a Vocabulary Word.**

7. You need money to buy goods at the _____

8. The area on a farm where animals stay is a _____.

 TRY THIS! Imagine that you are a cowboy or a cowgirl. Write a diary entry about a day in your life. Use as many of the Vocabulary Words as you can.

Name _____

Skill Reminder   **When you summarize, you tell what something is about. You should always use your own words to write a summary.**

▶ **Read each paragraph.**
Then write a summary.

Some birds are hunters. That means they prey, or feed, on smaller animals, insects, and plants. These birds include hawks, eagles, and falcons. The things that make each of these birds good hunters are very strong feet, an upper beak with a hook, and really good eyesight.

1. Summary: _____

_____

_____

_____

In North America there are 31 species of hawks, eagles, and falcons. They are found in plains, forests, deserts, and even cities.

2. Summary: _____

_____

_____

_____

Hawks, eagles, and falcons migrate each year during spring and fall. One place they travel is over the Goshute Mountains in Nevada. Visitors go to the top of these mountains and watch for these large birds. People find it educational and interesting to observe them.

3. Summary: _____

_____

_____

_____

The eagle is one of the largest birds in the world. Eagles fly high in the sky. Falcons are very powerful fliers, and they dive down from great heights to catch their prey. Hawks also swoop down and grab an animal with the claws on their feet.

4. Summary: _____

_____

_____

_____

Harcourt

Name _____

Skill Reminder   Use graphic sources as a means of displaying information.

▶ Imagine that you and your family are going to spend the day at Old West Town. Here is your schedule for the day. Use it to answer the questions that follow.

8:30–9:00	Drive to Old West Town
9:15–10:30	Go to western museum and see exhibits and a short movie
10:45–11:30	Watch cowboys in a riding and roping competition
11:45–12:45	Eat lunch around the campfire
1:15–3:00	Visit covered wagons and learn to lasso a horse
3:15–3:45	Return home

1. How many hours will you spend at Old West Town?

_____

2. How much time will you spend watching cowboys in a riding and

roping competition? _____

3. At what time will you leave your home to go to Old West Town?

_____

4. At what time will you leave Old West Town to return home?

_____

5. How much time will pass from when you finish eating to when you

visit the covered wagons? _____

6. Which activity takes the most amount of time?

_____

SCHOOL-HOME CONNECTION With your child, look through
newspapers or magazines for examples of graphic sources.
Discuss what the purpose of each graphic source is.

Harcourt

Name _____

▶ **Before you begin reading "Yippee-Yay!" complete the first two columns of this chart with what you know about cowboys and cowgirls and what you want to know about them. Then, after you finish reading, complete the third column.**

K What I Know	W What I Want to Know	L What I Learned

▶ **What was the most interesting thing you learned from reading "Yippee-Yay!"?**

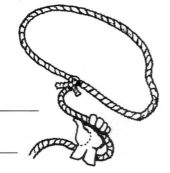

_____

_____

 TRY THIS! Imagine that you are a cowboy or a cowgirl. Write a paragraph describing the hardest part of your job.

Harcourt

▶ **Fill in each chart with the correct heads. Then complete the list of steps that describes how to use each one.**

K-W-L Strategy

1. _____	2. _____	3. _____
_____	_____	_____

4. First, I write down _____
5. In the next column, I write

_____

6. After I am finished reading, I list

_____

_____

SQ3R Strategy

7. _____	8. Here, I tell in a few words
9. _____ 10. In this column, I write _____ _____	11. _____ 12. To fill in this column, I _____ _____
13. _____ 14. After reading, I can _____	15. _____ 16. Then I use the chart to _____

Harcourt

▶ **Complete the poster for test-taking strategies.**

Things to Do Before a Test	Things to Do During a Test
1. Be sure you know _____ _____	**4.** Read all _____ _____
2. Study at the same _____ _____	**5.** Answer _____ _____
3. Get a good _____ _____	**6.** Go back to answer _____ _____
	7. If there is time, _____ _____

▶ **Rewrite each test-taking tip to make it correct.**

8. Start at the beginning and answer each question in order.

_____

_____

9. Read only the first set of directions. They will work for the whole test.

_____

_____

10. If you don't know the answer to a question, don't bother answering it.

_____

Harcourt

Name _____

▶ **Read the list of clothing names that come from other languages. Then fill in the labels on the picture.**

Clothing	Description	Origin
bandanna	square of cloth	India
beret	small, flat hat	France
kimono	robe	Japan
moccasin	soft leather shoe	U.S. (Native American)
serape	colorful woven shawl	Mexico
sombrero	wide-brimmed hat	Mexico
tote	carrying bag	Africa

1. _____

2. _____

3. _____

4. _____

5. _____

6. _____

7. _____

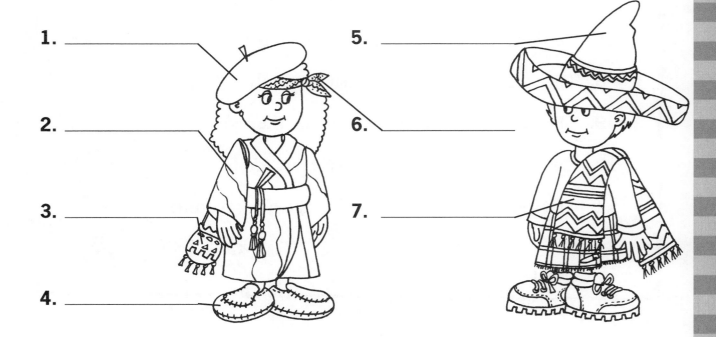

 TRY THIS! Create a menu that has the names of foods from other countries. Write a description of each dish.

Harcourt

Name _____

► **Draw a line under the verb in each sentence. Then write whether the verb is *present* or *past* tense.**

1. Cowboys worked on the plains. _____

2. Ranchers fenced part of their land. _____

3. The cattle wander over the fields. _____

4. All of the cowboys owned horses. _____

5. Today some cowboys use helicopters. _____

► **Complete each sentence with the correct past-tense form of the verb in parentheses ( ).**

6. The cattle _____ peacefully. **(graze)**

7. Cowboys _____ them up. **(round)**

8. They _____ the smallest calves. **(rope)**

9. The cattle _____ along. **(hurry)**

10. Lassos _____ every stray. **(grab)**

11. The trail boss _____ the herd. **(count)**

12. He _____ up all the branded cattle. **(add)**

Harcourt

TRY THIS! Use past-tense forms of the following words to write three sentences about a cowboy's day.   ***brand   trot   gaze***

Name _____

▶ **Write the Spelling Words from the box to complete the sentences.**

| leaving | hoping | taking | liked | getting | swimming |

I **(1)** _____ that movie. I kept **(2)** _____ the

good guys would win, and they did!

I'm really sad that you're **(3)** _____. We were just

(4) _____ to be friends.

It's too hot for us cowboys. How about **(5)** _____ a little

dip in that **(6)** _____ pool?

▶ **Write the Spelling Word that goes with each clue.**

| filled | shared | using | rolled |

7. rhymes with *paired* _____

8. rhymes with *bold* _____

9. rhymes with *refusing* _____

10. rhymes with *billed* _____

Handwriting Tip: When you write *d*, close the circle
so it doesn't look like *cl*. Write these words.

_____
_ _ _ _ _ _ _ _ _ _
d

11. rolled _____ **12.** shared _____

SCHOOL-HOME CONNECTION Make up sentences with your child,
using words that end in *-ed* and *-ing*. You can start with the Spelling Words
and then add other words, such as *promised, eating,* and *studying.*

Harcourt

Name _____

▶ **Complete each sentence with a word from the box.**

congratulations	earned	value	amount
receive	combinations	choices	

1. Did you _____ your prize yet?

2. Yes, I had three _____, and I chose this.

3. _____ on a great show.

4. Thanks. I spent a great _____ of time practicing.

5. There's more _____ in doing well than in winning a prize, don't you think?

6. Yes, but if you've _____ the prize, you should take it.

7. You can arrange your prizes in different _____ when you count them.

▶ **Complete the sentences with a Vocabulary Word.**

8. When you pick from many items, you have _____.

9. When someone wins a game or contest, you say words of

_____.

10. When you get something, you _____ it.

TRY THIS! What would you do if you had a million dollars? Write a paragraph telling about some of your plans. Use at least two of the Vocabulary Words.

Harcourt

Name _____

Skill Reminder Graphic sources make it easier to read certain types of information. Graphic sources include maps, diagrams, charts, tables, schedules, and time lines.

▶ Use the statements below to make a table or a graph.

Six people earn $18 selling baked goods.
Three people earn $30 washing cars.
One person earns $8 taking care of a neighbor's cat.
Six people earn $30 doing yard work.

▶ Answer these questions about the graph or table you made.

1. Which activity or activities earned the most amount of money?

_____

2. Which activity earned $12 less than washing cars?

_____

3. Which activity earned the least amount of money?

_____

4. What is the total amount of money earned? _____

 TRY THIS! Write a set of directions for making a table, a graph, or a time line. Then ask a partner to follow the directions and make the graphic aid.

Harcourt

Skill Reminder **A summary tells the main idea of a paragraph. It is written in your own words.**

▶ **Use the list of events below to write a summary.**

- Some Native Americans used copper plates as money.
- The Chinese once used small bronze tools for money.
- In Thailand and Alaska, types of beads and necklaces were used as money.
- The first coins made in Turkey were probably a bean-shaped mixture of gold and silver.

Summary: _____

_____

_____

▶ **Write a summary of the following paragraph.**

The United States trades goods with other countries. For example, it buys cars from Japan, cheese from France, and vegetables from South America. Since each country has its own form of money, when one country buys goods from another, it must first exchange its own money for an equal value of the other country's money. So, the United States can buy a Japanese car by trading its U.S. dollars for the Japanese yen.

_____

_____

SCHOOL-HOME CONNECTION With your child, ask family members about something they have done that they are proud of. Then write a summary of what they tell you.

Harcourt

Skill Reminder **When you compare, you look for things that are the same. When you contrast, you look for things that are different.**

▶ **Read each pair of sentences. Then choose the ending that best completes the second sentence. Write it on the line.**

1. Jason rode his bike to school. His brother, Ron, wanted to be just like his brother, so he _____.
   a. rode his bike to school, too   **b. took the bus to school**

2. Angela wore her hair in a ponytail. Her sister, Jean, wanted to be different from her sister, so she _____.
   a. wore her hair in a ponytail, too   **b. got her hair cut short**

3. Most of the people on Tulip Street planted tulips in their gardens, but the Jones family _____.
   a. also planted tulips   **b. planted daffodils instead**

4. Like the other clarinet players in the band, who practice on Saturday, Laurie _____.
   a. practices on Friday instead   **b. also practices on Saturday**

5. Brad likes Westerns; however, Joseph likes _____.
   a. comedies   **b. Westerns**

6. Lisa's favorite color is blue; likewise, Rae's favorite color is _____.
   a. blue   **b. red**

7. Tim and Tammy have the same amount of money. Tim has ten dimes, and Tammy has _____.
   a. ten dollars   **b. four quarters**

8. The twins want to look different, so Jo wears green and Flo wears _____.
   a. red   **b. green**

Harcourt

▶ Before you read "If You Made a Million," think about what you know about money. Then fill in the first two columns. Add to the second column while you read. Fill in the last column after you finish reading.

K	W	L
What I Know	**What I Want to Know**	**What I Learned**

▶ What is one new thing you learned about money in this selection?

_____

_____

_____

Harcourt

Name _____

Skill Reminder Everyday sources of information
include newspapers, magazines, maps, and advertisements.

▶ Refer to this map to answer the questions below.

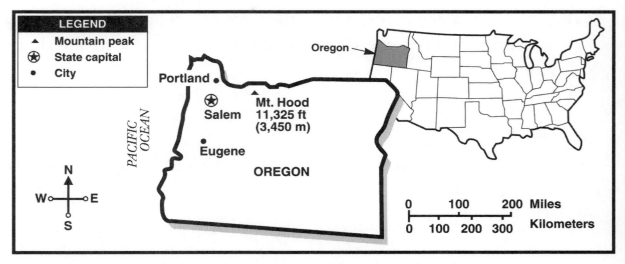

1. About how many miles is it across Oregon, from west to east?

_____

2. About how many miles is it from Portland to the southern border of

Oregon? _____

3. What is the capital of Oregon? _____

4. In which direction would you drive to get from Eugene to

Portland? _____

5. To get from Salem to Eugene, in which direction would you

drive? _____

6. In which part of the United States is Oregon—the northwest, the

southwest, the northeast, or the southeast? _____

7. What body of water touches Oregon's coast? _____

8. How tall is Mt. Hood, in feet? _____

TRY THIS! Make up five questions about your own state that could be answered
by looking at a map.

Harcourt

Name _____

Skill Reminder   **When you use your own words to
retell a story or part of a story, you are paraphrasing.**

▶ **Read each statement below. Then paraphrase it.**

1. If you have a dollar, it can be in the form of a dollar bill, four quarters,
   ten dimes, twenty nickels, a hundred pennies, or many combinations of
   these coins.

   _____

   _____

2. You can carry around a roll of quarters, which has 40 quarters in it, or
   a ten-dollar bill.

   _____

   _____

3. If you keep your money in a bank for 20 years, you'll get more interest
   than if you keep it in a bank for 15 years, 10 years, 5 years, or 1 year.

   _____

   _____

4. Once you've earned a lot of money, you have to figure out
   whether to spend it or save it.

   _____

   _____

5. Once you have a million dollars in a bank, you can collect
   approximately $1,000 a week in interest.

   _____

   _____

6. A bank gets the money to lend to people by using the
   money other people have put in the bank to save.

   _____

   _____

Harcourt

Name _____

▶ **On the lines below, write the shortened, more familiar form of the underlined words.**

1. I'd buy a new red automobile.

2. I'd take a taxicab everywhere I wanted to go.

3. Our house needs new draperies.

4. We ate a submarine sandwich.

5. I'd buy a new condominium for my grandmother.

6. "I'd buy a gasoline station for my uncle," said Ben.

7. Heather said, "I've always wanted a limousine."

8. "I think I'd get a big airplane," said Kwang.

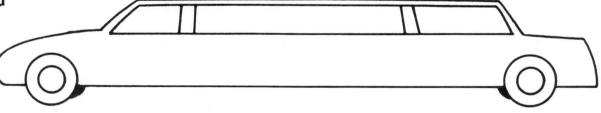

1. _____   **5.** _____

2. _____   **6.** _____

3. _____   **7.** _____

4. _____   **8.** _____

 TRY THIS! Imagine you are taking a vacation away from home. Write a postcard to a friend, telling about what you've been doing. Use some clipped words in your message.

Harcourt

Name _____

▶ **Draw one line under the present-tense verbs.
Draw two lines under the past-tense verbs.**

1. You have one million dollars in nickels.

2. "Awesome!" says your uncle.

3. "You clearly did something right."

4. He saw your stacks of nickels.

5. Now he comes to the bank with you.

▶ **Rewrite each sentence, using the correct past-tense or present-tense
form of the verb in parentheses ( ).**

6. A money truck _____ down the street. **(come)**

_____

7. The driver has _____ the bank. **(see)**

_____

8. "There's the entrance," he _____. **(say)**

_____

9. They have _____ with bags of cash. **(come)**

_____

10. The guards have _____ a long day. **(have)**

_____

TRY THIS! Use past-tense forms of these verbs to write three sentences about visiting a bank. *have, come, see*

Harcourt

Name _____

▶ **Write the Spelling Word from the box that best completes each sentence.**

question	section	motion	permission	vacation	attention

1. Harry got _____ to go to the fair.

2. The _____ of the Ferris wheel gave Harry a thrill.

3. Harry went to the _____ where the animals were.

4. He had a _____ to ask the owner of a cow.

5. "How much _____ does a cow need?" he asked.

6. "Well," said the owner, "I couldn't go away on _____ this year."

▶ **Write these Spelling Words in alphabetical order.**

vision	action	confusion	nation

7. _____   9. _____

8. _____   10. _____

Handwriting Tip: Do not loop an *i*, or it may look like an *e*. Write these words.

_____
i

11. attention _____   12. vacation _____

SCHOOL-HOME CONNECTION With your child, take turns making up sentences with words that end with -tion or -sion. Try to make the sentences go together to tell a story.

Journeys of Wonder   **91**

Name _____

▶ **Finish this letter. Use words from the box to complete the sentences.**

signal	celebrations	choosy	average	tracks	bloom

Dear Grandpa,

    I've been in the desert for a month now. I find it quite interesting.

Delicate flowers **(1)** _____ on the cactus plants. I see the

(2) _____ of wild animals, like coyotes and hares. Sometimes I follow them to see where they lead.

    Yesterday I saw two cactus plants that seemed to be reaching out to shake

hands with each other. I think they were trying to **(3)** _____ to me that the desert is really a friendly place. Some sunsets are just

(4) _____, but yesterday I saw a special one. I am fairly

(5) _____ about what I call "special," as you know.

    Soon I will be home. There will be **(6)** _____ to welcome me back, I know. Then I will tell you all about the other things I saw in the desert.

                    Your granddaughter,

                    Alicia

Harcourt

▶ **Complete each sentence with a Vocabulary Word.**

7. Animals and people leave _____ when they walk.

8. People all around the world have _____.

Name _____

Skill Reminder **Authors have a purpose for writing. It may be to inform, to entertain, or to persuade.**

▶ **Read each paragraph below. Then tell whether the author's purpose is to inform, to entertain, or to persuade.**

Imagine yourself walking in a hot and very dry place. Everywhere around, you see sand and more sand. You spy a cactus in the distance and see iguanas, gila monsters, and even an armadillo. You are in a desert.

1. The author's purpose for writing is to _____.

2. How do you know? _____

_____

Did you know that rain forests are in great danger? Every day, thousands of square meters of land are destroyed by people. The animals and plants that live in this habitat are being destroyed, too. People need to stop harming rain forests. They should think about protecting them before they no longer exist, and the plants and animals living there become extinct.

3. The author's purpose for writing is _____

_____.

4. How do you know? _____

_____

_____

Once upon a time, there was a coyote who wanted to be a bird. He asked each bird to give him a feather. The coyote figured out a way to attach the feathers to his back, and he tried to fly. Just imagine what a sight a coyote with flapping feathers must have been!

5. The author's purpose is _____.

6. How do you know? _____

_____

Name _____

Skill Reminder Figurative language is language that helps you picture in your mind what's happening.

▶ **Read each sentence beginning, and choose which phrase best completes it.**

1. The cactus was as prickly as _____.

   a pincushion **a piece of silk** **a carrot**

2. The whirlwinds seemed to be as tall _____.

   as a valley **as the grass** **as a skyscraper**

3. The drizzling rain was as gentle as _____.

   a lion **a baby lamb** **a thunderstorm**

4. The jackrabbit was sitting on his hind legs, as still as _____.

   a rock **a waterfall** **the wind**

5. The cloud was as pink as _____.

   a shark **a flamingo** **the grass**

6. The coyote moved as silently as _____.

   a herd of elephants **children on a playground** **the moon**

▶ **Choose the answer in Column B that best finishes the phrase in Column A. Write the letter on the line.**

A	B
1. smooth as _____	a. a growing seed
2. quiet as _____	b. sandpaper
3. colorful as _____	c. silk
4. rough as _____	d. a rainbow

Harcourt

Name _____

▶ **Complete the Time Line/Sequence Chart below.
List the dates and celebrations in the order in which
they are mentioned in the story.**

Date	Celebration

▶ **Why isn't the author lonely in the desert?**

_____

_____

_____

 TRY THIS! Write about something you have seen in nature that made you stop and wonder. If you haven't seen something extraordinary, write about something in nature that interests you. Then give it a name to remember it by.

Harcourt

Name _____

▶ **Read the paragraph. Then fill in the word web to show the important details.**

Many African Americans celebrate the holiday of Kwanzaa. Did you know that it once was a celebration of the first fruits of the winter? Today, Kwanzaa celebrates family, culture, and community. It is a seven-day celebration that begins on December 26. Each day, families light a candle and discuss ideas of African American culture. People in communities also sing, dance, recite poetry, and eat special foods. This celebration honors the achievements of African Americans.

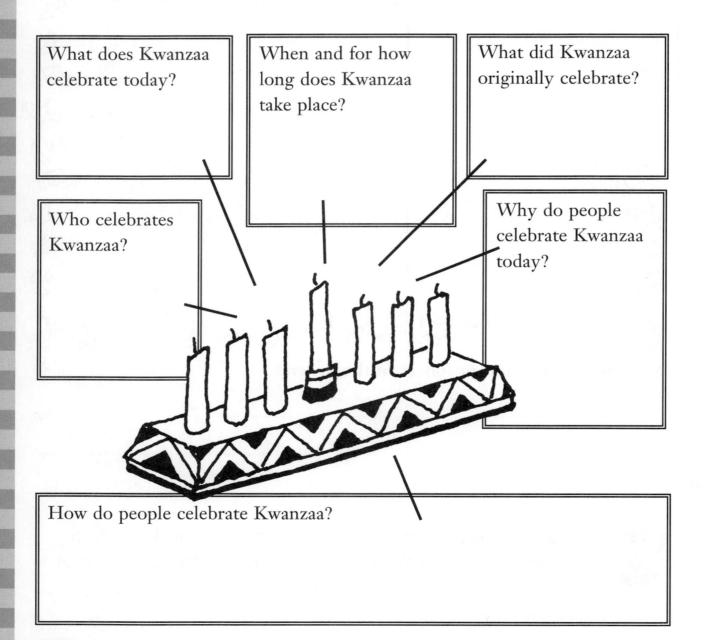

What does Kwanzaa celebrate today?

When and for how long does Kwanzaa take place?

What did Kwanzaa originally celebrate?

Who celebrates Kwanzaa?

Why do people celebrate Kwanzaa today?

How do people celebrate Kwanzaa?

Harcourt

Name _____

▶ **Read the passage and then answer the questions. Fill in the oval next to your choice.**

People celebrate holidays. Mexicans and Mexican Americans, for example, celebrate Cinco de Mayo, "the fifth of May," to honor the defenders of Mexican freedom. The Chinese have a New Year's festival during late January or early February that lasts for fifteen days. Rosh Hashanah is the Jewish New Year. It is observed for two days during September or October. And, of course, January 1, New Year's Day, is celebrated by many people throughout the world.

1 What is the main idea of this passage?
- ⬭ New Year's Day is fun.
- ⬭ Chinese New Year lasts for fifteen days.
- ⬭ People everywhere celebrate holidays.
- ⬭ Cinco de Mayo is on May 5.

2 Who celebrates Cinco de Mayo?
- ⬭ Mexicans and Mexican Americans
- ⬭ Chinese
- ⬭ Jews
- ⬭ people everywhere

3 What is Rosh Hashanah?
- ⬭ a day in February
- ⬭ a celebration during May
- ⬭ Jewish New Year
- ⬭ Chinese New Year

4 When is Rosh Hashanah celebrated?
- ⬭ in May
- ⬭ in December
- ⬭ in September or October
- ⬭ on January 1

5 When is the Chinese New Year celebrated?
- ⬭ during May
- ⬭ during late January or early February
- ⬭ during September or October
- ⬭ on January 1

6 Why do people celebrate Cinco de Mayo?
- ⬭ to honor the defenders of Mexican freedom
- ⬭ to honor Chinese heritage
- ⬭ to celebrate traditions
- ⬭ to celebrate family

Harcourt

Name _____

▶ **Write two words from the box that are related to each word below.**

windy	**direction**	**perfectly**	**whirlwind**
perfection	**creature**	**signal**	**indirect**
creative	**memorize**	**assignment**	**unwrap**
myself	**wrapper**	**remember**	**selfish**

wind

_____

_____

perfect

_____

_____

create

_____

_____

sign

_____

_____

wrap

_____

_____

self

_____

_____

direct

_____

_____

memory

_____

_____

TRY THIS! Look in a science book for a long word. Look it up in a dictionary. On a sheet of paper, write any word parts or related words you know.

Harcourt

Name _____

▶ **Rewrite each sentence. Change present-tense verbs to
past tense. Change past-tense verbs to present tense.**

1. I give each day a name.

_____

2. Today I rode in a pickup truck.

_____

3. Seven dust devils went by.

_____

4. I take pictures of these things.

_____

5. I write about special days in my journal.

_____

▶ **Complete each sentence, using the correct past-tense
form of the verb in parentheses ( ).**

6. Later, I _____ down the canyon. **(go)**

7. I always _____ a sketchpad with me. **(take)**

8. Once, I had _____ a picture of a hawk. **(take)**

9. The hawk had _____ on the wind. **(rode)**

10. Then it _____ something in the field. **(eat)**

TRY THIS! Use past-tense forms of the verbs *go*, *ride*, and *take*. Write three
sentences about a place you like to visit.

Harcourt

Name _____

► **Write the Spelling Words to complete the sentences.**

softly	useful	thankful	lonely	farmer	suitable

A tractor can be very **(1)** _____ to a **(2)** _____.

If corn could talk, it would be **(3)** _____ for the rain that falls

(4) _____. Farming can be a very **(5)** _____ job. It

is not **(6)** _____ work for people who like big cities.

► **Match a word from the box to each definition.**

readable	teacher	quietly	exactly

7. without sound _____

8. just right _____

9. easy to read _____

10. person who teaches _____

Handwriting Tip: Form the lower loop of an *f* correctly, so it doesn't look like a *b*. Write these words.

11. softly _____

12. thankful _____

SCHOOL-HOME CONNECTION With your child, find items in your home that can be described with words ending in -er, -ful, -ly, and -able. Make up sentences using these words. Here is an example: This shirt is *washable*.

Harcourt

Name _____

▶ **Complete each sentence with a word from the box.**

| windmill | cherished | furrows | ample | shunned | growth |

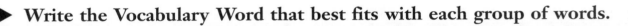

1. One step in making a garden is plowing _____ in the ground.

2. To have healthy plants, use _____ amounts of water.

3. A _____ can help pump water from a well.

4. A _____ garden is one that is well cared for.

5. Lately, some gardeners have _____ the use of poisons in their gardens.

6. Sunshine and rain help the plants' _____.

▶ **Write the Vocabulary Word that best fits with each group of words.**

7. enough
   plenty of

   _____

8. stayed away from
   avoided

   _____

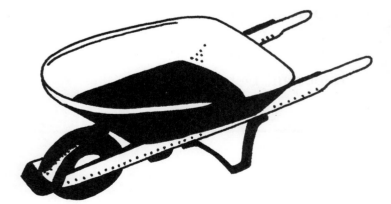

Harcourt

SCHOOL-HOME CONNECTION With your child, role-play an interview with a gardener or farmer. You can play the interviewer and your child can play the guest, or vice versa.

Journeys of Wonder **101**

Name _____

Skill Reminder **The important details in a paragraph tell more about the main idea.**

▶ **Read the paragraph. Then complete the chart by writing the important details in the chart.**

Animals that live in the deserts of the southwestern United States have to make the most of what little water is available to them. A few of the animals, such as the pocket mouse and the pack rat, can survive without drinking very  often. Some animals, such as the desert tortoise, get enough to drink from the prickly pear cactus. Other animals, such as the kit fox, are able to go for long periods without water and then get enough water for their needs from one drinking session.

Main Idea: Animals that live in the southwestern U.S. have to make the most of what little water is available to them.
Important Details
Important Detail:
Important Detail:
Important Detail:

Harcourt

Name _____

Skill Reminder   Each part of a book has a special
purpose. Knowing how to use the parts of a book can help
you quickly locate information.

▶ Use the words in the box to identify in which parts of a book the
information below can be found.

title page	table of contents	
copyright page	glossary	index

1. *Alejandro's Gift*
by Richard E. Albert
Illustrated by Sylvia Long
Chronicle Books
San Francisco

_____

2. Before you read 9
Alejandro's Gift 11
Rocking and Rolling 25

_____

3. Text Copyright © 1994
by Richard E. Albert.
Illustration Copyright
© 1994 by Sylvia Long.

_____

4. bats, 114
bees, 26
birds, 171
bugs, 2

_____

▶ In which book part would you find answers to these questions?

5. What is the meaning of *saguaro*? _____

6. What people are found in the book? _____

7. On what page does Chapter 6 begin? _____

8. Who is the author of the book? _____

TRY THIS!   Write three questions about a topic, such as the desert. Ask a partner
to tell which book parts he or she would use to find the answers.

Harcourt

▶ As you read "Alejandro's Gift," complete the problem-solving chart below. Remember to think about what Alejandro's problem is and what he does that helps solve the problem.

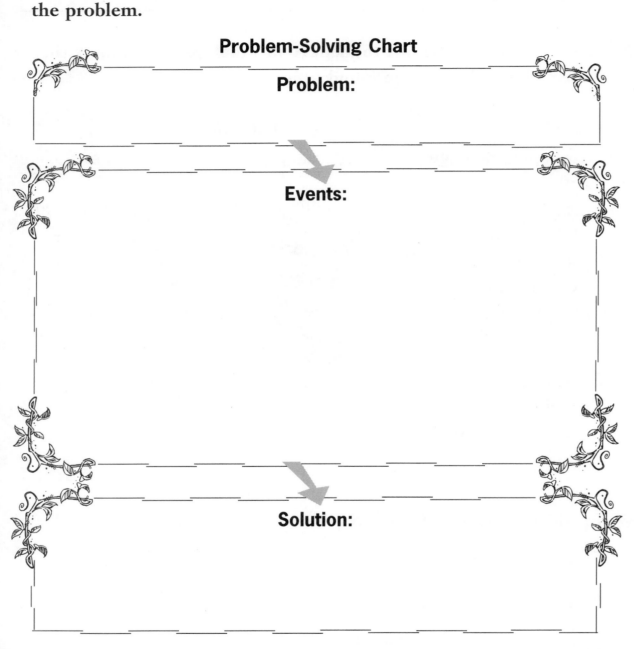

Problem-Solving Chart

Problem:

Events:

Solution:

▶ Why do you think the animals didn't go to Alejandro's first water hole to get water?

_____

_____

Harcourt

Name _____

▶ **Read the paragraph. Then answer the questions.**

> You are a pioneer who has to travel long distances over a rugged trail. There are many others who want to make the same journey as well. No one is certain how or when it is best to travel. How will you and the others make and survive the journey?

1. What is the main problem? _____

2. What information is given that might be important?

_____

_____

3. What other things might it be helpful to know to make a plan?

_____

_____

4. What is one way you might solve the problem?

_____

5. What might be another solution to the problem?

_____

6. Which solution do you think is the best? Explain why.

_____

_____

 TRY THIS! Think of a problem you have had to solve recently. Make a list of things you did to solve it. Discuss your choices.

Name _____

▶ **Read the paragraph. Then complete the sentences below for each underlined word.**

Agriculture is the science of growing crops. When a farmer plants a crop, he uses machines. A tractor is used to pull a plow. A plow turns the soil and makes deep grooves, or furrows, for planting seeds. Barley, oats, and wheat are crops called grains. Machines called drills are used to plant grains. Drills cut the soil into furrows, drop in the seeds, and cover the seeds all at one time. When the crop is grown, a harvesting machine, or reaper, cuts the crop, and a thresher helps separate and collect it.

1. *Agriculture* is the science of _____.

2. A *tractor* is a _____.

3. A *plow* _____.

4. *Furrow* means _____.

5. Crops that are *grains* are _____.

6. *Drills* are used to plant _____.

7. A *reaper* is a machine that is used to _____.

8. A *thresher* _____.

TRY THIS! Think of two more words that tell about something you can do on a farm. Use those words in sentences that describe the activities.

Harcourt

Name _____

▶ **Underline the forms of the verb *be*. Write whether each is *present* or *past* tense.**

1. Alejandro was a kind man. _____

2. The animals were pleased with his gift. _____

3. Now he is less lonely. _____

4. The animals are happier, too. _____

5. I am glad for all of them. _____

▶ **Rewrite each sentence, using the form of *be* given in parentheses ( ).**

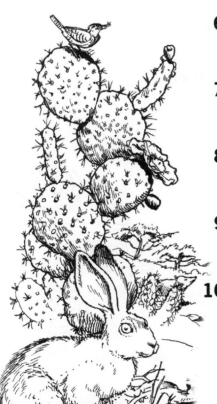

6. You _____ rarely alone. **(present)**

_____

7. He _____ with his friends. **(present)**

_____

8. I _____ a friendly person. **(present)**

_____

9. He _____ lonely for his family. **(past)**

_____

10. They _____ far away. **(past)**

_____

Harcourt

SCHOOL-HOME CONNECTION With your child, ask family members for words they would use to describe themselves—for example, *smart, young, active*. Write a sentence for each person, using a form of *be* and a describing word.

Name _____

▶ **Write Spelling Words from the box to complete the story.**

pennies	buried	replied	married	emptied	studied

I found a box in the garden. It had been **(1)** _____ in the

ground long ago. It was full of old nickels and **(2)** _____.

I brought it in and **(3)** _____ the coins out on the table.

I **(4)** _____ the dates on them. I told my dad about it. He

(5) _____, "I guess your great-grandpa put them there. That

was about the time he and your great-grandma got **(6)** _____."

▶ **Write a Spelling Word from the box to match each clue.**

candies	stories	copies	parties

7. does the same thing _____

8. sweets _____

9. celebrations _____

10. tales _____

Handwriting Tip: Be sure to dot an *i*. Write these words.

i

11. pennies _____   **12.** stories _____

Harcourt

SCHOOL-HOME CONNECTION With your child, add *-es* or *-ed* to these words, changing the *y* to *i*: *carry*, *worry*, *supply*, and *try*. Use each new word in a sentence.

Name _____

▶ **Choose from the words on the mountains. Write the word that answers each riddle.**

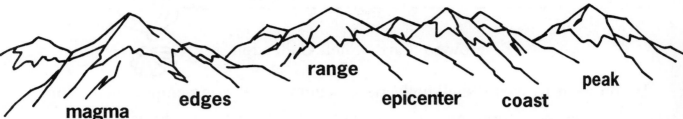

range

peak

edges   epicenter   coast

magma

1. I am the outside borders of something, not the center of it.

What am I? the _____

2. I am another word for a group of mountains.

What am I? a _____

3. I am melted rock beneath the surface of the earth.

What am I? _____

4. I am the top of a mountain. What am I?

a _____

5. I am the place where the ocean meets the land. What am I?

the _____

6. I am the place where an earthquake starts. What am I?

the _____

▶ **Complete the paragraph with Vocabulary Words.**

Sally hiked on the mountain **(7)** _____ near the **(8)** _____

of California. As she reached a **(9)** _____, or the top of a

mountain, she could see an erupting volcano. She would get a lot of

great pictures up there.

TRY THIS! Write a paragraph comparing land that is flat and land that is not flat. Use some of the Vocabulary Words.

Name _____

Skill Reminder **When you read, look for the important details that support the main idea of the paragraph.**

How to Start a Shell Collection

If you want to start a shell collection, begin by collecting empty shells from places like beaches, ponds and streams. Wash the shells to get rid of any dirt or other matter. Then, put your shells into groups, and label them. You can use a box to display your shells. Just take a large box, and divide it into sections by using cardboard. Next, place cotton in each section. Use rectangles of cardboard for labels, and attach a label to each section. Finally, put the shells in the correct section and place each on top of the cotton.

Remember, never include a living shelled animal in your collection. Always put a living shelled animal back where you found it.

1. What is this paragraph about? _____

2. What details should you follow to start a shell collection?

_____

_____

_____

3. Where can you find shells? _____

_____

4. Why should you wash your shells? _____

_____

5. What is one thing you should never include in a shell collection?

_____

6. What should you do with a living shelled animal?

_____

Harcourt

Name _____

Skill Reminder When reading nonfiction, you can use
Study Strategies such as K-W-L, QAR, and SQRRR.

▶ Complete the headings for this study-strategy chart. Then answer
the question.

K-W-L		
What I Already	What I	What I
1. _____	2. _____	3. _____

4. How does K-W-L help you study and learn new information?

_____

_____

_____

▶ **Rewrite the following step for SQRRR in the correct order.**

Recite: In this step, I read aloud the information I wrote down.

Survey: I preview the article or chapter and write what I think it will be about.

Read: I read to find answers to the questions and write them in the chart.

Question: I turn the subheads in the article or chapter into questions.

Review: I reread or review all the new information I have learned.

5. _____

_____

6. _____

_____

7. _____

_____

8. _____

9. _____

Harcourt

Name _____

▶ Before you read "Rocking and Rolling," think about what you know about the Earth, earthquakes, mountains, and erosion. Then fill in the first two columns. Add to the second column while you read. Fill in the last column after you finish reading.

K What I Know	W What I Want to Know	L What I Learned

▶ What is the most important thing you learned from reading "Rocking and Rolling"?

_____

_____

_____

Name _____

▶ **Think about "Rocking and Rolling." Write the cause or the effect in the chart below.**

Cause	Effect
1. The Earth's plates crunch into one another.	
2.	Block mountains are formed.
3. Magma bulges up beneath the crust.	
4.	An earthquake occurs.
5. Erosion happens.	
6. Rocks in a river rubbed against the land.	

▶ **Think of another cause and its effect on the Earth that you read in "Rocking and Rolling." Write the cause and the effect in the boxes.**

Cause	Effect
7.	**8.**

TRY THIS! Think of things you do that affect the Earth. Write two cause-and-effect sentences about these things. For example, "I plant flowers because I want the world to look beautiful."

Harcourt

Name _____

▶ **Read the paragraphs. Then choose the best answer.
Fill in the circle next to your choice.**

Earthquakes can cause damage and destruction. Some earthquakes are too small to be felt, but others are so strong that they change the way the Earth looks. An earthquake in 1985 in Mexico City destroyed hundreds of buildings. Thousands of people lost their lives and their homes, and many schools and other buildings collapsed.

Earthquakes take place in the Earth's crust—the rocks inside the Earth. There are cracks, or faults, in the rocks. Energy builds up when the rocks on one side of a fault push against the rocks on the other side. This pushing has caused the Earth to crack into pieces called plates. The plates move, and they slide under or pull away from each other. Sometimes one plate hits another plate, and so an earthquake happens.

Scientists have learned to measure movements along the faults in the Earth. However, they can't predict weeks or even days before when an earthquake will happen.

1 Which of these is a cause of an earthquake?
- ⬭ a bridge collapsing
- ⬭ the faults in the Earth's crust
- ⬭ a plate hitting another plate
- ⬭ the shaping of the Earth

2 What was an effect of the earthquake that occurred in Mexico City in 1985?
- ⬭ buildings were safe
- ⬭ people lost their lives and their homes
- ⬭ a tsunami occurred
- ⬭ scientists learned to measure the Earth's movement

3 Which one of these words gives you a clue to causes and effects?
- ⬭ when
- ⬭ but
- ⬭ and so
- ⬭ then

4 What happens when an earthquake is strong?
- ⬭ the way the Earth looks is changed
- ⬭ the land becomes more fertile
- ⬭ winds become strong
- ⬭ the Earth feels solid and firm

Harcourt

Name ___ _____

▶ **Write the word you would look up in a computer database or in the card catalog of your local library in order to find the answers to the questions below.**

1. What causes earthquakes? _____

2. Where are the Himalayas? _____

3. What are the differences among fold mountains, block mountains, and dome mountains?

   _____

4. How do glaciers change the land? _____

5. How was the Grand Canyon in Arizona formed?

   _____

6. What other books has Phillip Steele written?

   _____

7. What happened to the island of Krakatoa?

   _____

8. What are some other books about how soil is formed?

   _____

9. What animals might live on the tundra? _____

10. What happened when Mount Saint Helens erupted?

    _____

 TRY THIS! Look up one of the topics above in an encyclopedia and write a brief report on it.

▶ **Write the homograph from the picture that completes each sentence. Use each homograph twice.**

1. We went to see a _____ concert that was outdoors near a mountain.

2. The singer wore a large

   _____ in her hair.

3. A _____ flew down onto the stage.

4. The singer was frightened

   and _____ under a chair.

5. When she was done, she

   took a _____ .

6. My family visited a state park

   near where we _____ .

7. "What time is it?" my mother

   asked. "I forgot to _____ my watch."

8. We drove through the _____ and looked at the cactuses.

9. I was ready to _____ our house and camp outdoors.

10. On the way home, we put the car top down. We could feel the

    _____ in our hair.

wind

bow

live

dove

desert

Harcourt

Name _____

▶ **Write the two words that make up each contraction.**

1. Isn't the earth always changing? _____

2. We're studying earth science in school. _____

3. I think it's very interesting. _____

4. Volcanoes don't erupt often. _____

5. Earthquakes aren't common, either. _____

▶ **Rewrite each sentence using a contraction in place of the underlined words.**

6. You <u>could not</u> walk to the center of the earth.

_____

_____

7. Earth's plates <u>do not</u> stay still.

_____

8. <u>They are</u> always moving.

_____

9. You <u>can not</u> feel the earth move.

_____

10. <u>I am</u> sure that is true.

_____

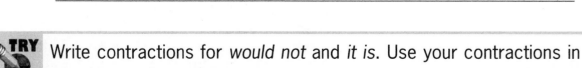

TRY THIS! Write contractions for *would not* and *it is*. Use your contractions in sentences of your own.

Harcourt

Name _____

► **Write a Spelling Word from the box to complete
each sentence.**

| didn't | we've | it's | she's | haven't |

(1) _____ called the Transamerica Building, but it looks like

a pyramid. (2) _____ you say that you went to the top floor?

My aunt works there. (3) _____ worked there for two years.

(4) _____ got an hour before the tour bus leaves. I (5) _____

seen a building like this before.

► **Write the Spelling Word that fits each shape.**

| you've | he'd | they'd |

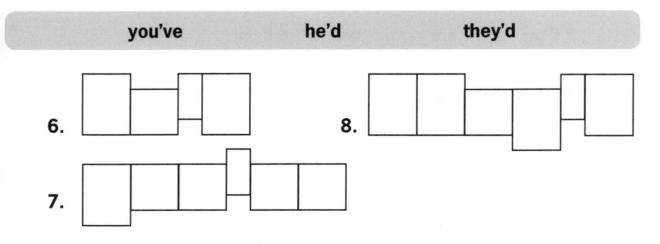

6.

7.

8.

Handwriting Tip: Leave space for an apostrophe in a word
that needs one. Write these words.

he'd

9. isn't _____   **11.** we'd _____

10. you've _____   **12.** didn't _____

SCHOOL-HOME CONNECTION With your child, look through ads, catalogs, and
flyers for words with contractions. Tell each other what the words would be without
the contraction. For example, if you find the word *she'd,* say "she would" or "she had."

Harcourt

Name _____

▶ **Complete the puzzle by matching a word to each definition below. Choose from the words in the box.**

eventually	entire	continent	sphere	universe	homeward

ACROSS

2. a shape like a ball

5. after a long time; finally

6. everything that exists

DOWN

1. all; the whole thing

3. toward the place where you live

4. a big land area on the earth

▶ **Solve these riddles with Vocabulary Words.**

7. A snowball is in the shape of a _____.

8. North America, a large body of land, is a _____.

TRY THIS! Imagine you can fly anywhere you want to go, like a bird. Write about what you see on one of your flights. Use at least two of the Vocabulary Words.

Harcourt

Name _____

Skill Reminder **The reason something happens is a cause. What happens is the effect.**

▶ **For each of the following sentences, write the cause in the box on the left. Write the effect in the box on the right.**

1. The armadillo was curious about the world, so he decided to take a trip.

Cause: _____ Effect: _____

2. Because he traveled northeast, he soon reached San Antonio.

Cause: _____ Effect: _____

3. A jackrabbit was so frightened that he ran away.

Cause: _____ Effect: _____

4. The eagle flew high so he could see far in all directions.

Cause: _____ Effect: _____

5. In order not to fall off, Armadillo held on tight.

Cause: _____ Effect: _____

6. The prairie was dry because it hadn't rained in a long time.

Cause: _____ Effect: _____

Harcourt

Skill Reminder Problem solving involves exploring a
problem, gathering information about possible solutions, and
using judgment to choose the best solution.

▶ Read the weather forecast. Then answer the questions below.

Weather in the Amarillo area tomorrow
will be cloudy with a 90% chance of
rain by mid-morning. Rain is expected
to continue all day. The ground is
already holding as much water as
possible. Therefore, this additional rain
is expected to cause flooding in some
areas. Residents are advised to avoid
traveling, stay home if possible, and
await further word.

The armadillo from Amarillo is planning to start a trip tomorrow.
What is the problem with this plan?

1. _____

_____

What are three choices the armadillo has?

2. _____

3. _____

4. _____

What do you think is the best choice?

5. _____

Why do you think this is the best choice?

6. _____

Harcourt

Name _____

▶ Fill in the sequence chart below as you read "The Armadillo from Amarillo." Remember to list the events in the order in which they appear in the story.

Place	Event

▶ What was the question Sasparillo wondered about before he started his journey, and what was his answer at the end of the journey?

_____

_____

_____

Harcourt

Name _____

Skill Reminder Pronouns such as *he, she, it,* or *they* or
other words such as *where* or *that* often refer to
characters, places, or things that were already
mentioned.

▶ **Write the word or words that each underlined
word in the sentences refers to.**

The armadillo was excited to be traveling
around Texas. <u>He</u> liked <u>where</u> he was now.

1. He: _____

2. where: _____
In San Antonio the armadillo saw the Alamo.
<u>It's</u> a fort where a battle took place.

3. It's: _____
San Antonio also has a beautiful Riverwalk.
People can dine and shop in the stores located
<u>here</u>. <u>They</u> can also take boat rides and view
the scenery.

4. here: _____

5. They: _____
The armadillo found out that Texas is a huge
state. <u>It</u> has many cities, people, and things to
do. Once <u>he</u> took a ride on the back of an eagle.
<u>He</u> and the armadillo went up into the sky to
see everything the world around them had to offer.

6. It: _____

7. he: _____

8. He: _____

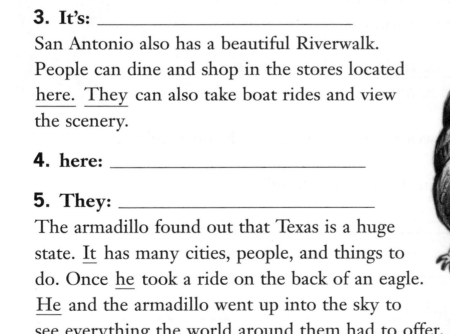

Harcourt

Name _____

▶ **Write the word that stands for the underlined word or words in each sentence.**

1. Some <u>explorers</u> came to Texas from Spain. _____ settled near El Paso in 1682.

2. In 1871, about 700,000 cattle were led from Texas to <u>Abilene</u>, Kansas. _____ is a large railroad shipping center.

3. Amarillo, a large city in Texas, is known for many <u>products</u>. Oil is one of _____.

4. One <u>company</u> that sells cattle is in Amarillo. _____ is called the Amarillo Livestock Auction Company.

5. <u>Armadillo</u> lived in Texas, but _____ wanted to see the rest of the world.

6. <u>Armadillo and the eagle</u> saw the moon as _____ traveled in a spaceship.

▶ **Write one possible word for each of the referents below.**

7. Dad, Mom, Cousin Brillo, and Grandpa: _____

8. the armadillo: _____

9. Texas: _____

10. the soaring eagles: _____

TRY THIS! Write a riddle using some words that stand for other words. Then ask a partner to solve your riddle.

Harcourt

Name _____

▶ In this puzzle, find eight more words that rhyme with
grain. Circle them and then write them on the lines.
Words can be found horizontally, vertically, or diagonally.

```
P  L  A  I  N  V  A  J  E  C
X  M  M  R  T  C  A  N  E  R
L  B  L  A  Z  F  P  D  D  A
A  R  G  L  N  A  A  T  P  N
N  R  A  A  B  E  N  S  A  E
E  E  A  I  I  I  E  U  I  C
O  T  R  A  I  N  G  J  N  K
```

1. _____plain_____   6. _____

2. _____rain_____   7. _____

3. _____   8. _____

4. _____   9. _____

5. _____   10. _____

TRY THIS! Create a rhyming poem using some of the words you found.

Harcourt

Name _____

▶ **Underline the verb. Circle the adverb that describes it.**

1. The armadillo lands shakily.

2. He sits down with a sigh.

3. The eagle flaps his beautiful wings again.

4. The armadillo waves wearily.

5. Then he closes his eyes.

▶ **Write whether the underlined adverb tells** *where,* *when,* **or** *how.*

6. Together we fly into the sky. _____

7. We see all of Texas below. _____

8. Now I can see Mexico. _____

9. It shimmers brightly in the sun. _____

10. We return to earth afterward. _____

▶ **Choose two sentences from 6–10 above. Rewrite each sentence you choose, using a different adverb.**

11. _____

12. _____

TRY THIS! Think of three adverbs that could tell *where,* *when,* and *how* about the underlined verb below. Rewrite the sentence three times, using your adverbs.

The little armadillo napped.

Harcourt

Name _____

▶ **Write Spelling Words from the box to complete the sentences.**

over	never	river	tower

The airplane ride was exciting. I could see the

(1) _____ that flows past my

house. I **(2)** _____ knew it

could look so small! We flew **(3)** _____ mountains and

plains. Then, people in a control **(4)** _____ at the airport
told the pilot when to land.

▶ **Match a Spelling Word to each clue.**

water	under	rather	finger

5. not over _____

6. prefer _____

7. It's wet. _____

8. part of a hand _____

Handwriting Tip: Be careful a written *r* does not look
like a *v*. Write these words.

_____

_____
 r

9. wonder _____

10. number _____

SCHOOL-HOME CONNECTION With your child, look
around your home for things whose names end in -er—
for example, *number, sprinkler, mower, juicer, toaster.*

Journeys of Wonder **127**

Harcourt

Name _____

▶ **Write the word that matches the definition. Choose from the words in the box.**

| force | nucleus | loops |
| solar wind | particles | fluorescent |

1. a blowing force from the sun _____

2. the center of something _____

3. glowing brightly _____

4. power or energy _____

5. what an object makes when it moves in a curved line that

crosses over itself again and again _____

6. very small pieces _____

▶ **Write the Vocabulary Word that best completes each set of words.**

7. bits
pieces

_____

8. center
middle

_____

SCHOOL-HOME CONNECTION With your child, make
up a riddle about each Vocabulary Word—for example,
I am strong. I can move things. What am I? (force)

Harcourt

Name _____

Skill Reminder The reason something happens is a cause. What happens is the effect.

▶ **Read each effect below. Then choose the most probable cause for each one. Write it on the line.**

1. Effect: Jan H. Oort became an astronomer.

Cause: _____

He was interested in the stars.   He wanted to be an actor.

2. Effect: A comet moves toward the Sun.

Cause: _____

The Sun's heat attracts it.   The Sun's gravity attracts it.

3. Effect: The tails of a comet always point away from the Sun.

Cause: _____

The planets pull them.   The solar wind pushes them away.

4. Effect: The Moon and the planets shine.

Cause: _____

They reflect sunlight.   They glow from within.

▶ **The items in the box are effects. The numbered items are causes. On the line next to each cause, write the effect that goes with it.**

I went to sleep.	**I put on a sweater.**
I had to run to the bus stop.	**I woke up.**

5. I was very tired. _____

6. The alarm clock went off at 6:30. _____

7. I got out of the house late. _____

8. I was cold. _____

Harcourt

Name _____

Skill Reminder To find answers to questions you have about any topic, you can do research. The library and the Internet are two places you can begin your research.

▶ You want to write a report about a topic such as comets and meteors. What steps might you take to research the topic? Complete the flowchart to show what you should do. Use as many details as you can in the flowchart.

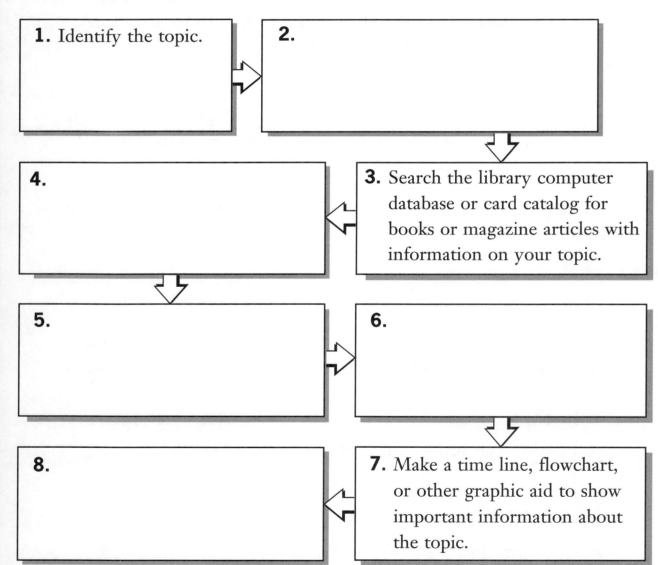

1. Identify the topic.

2.

3. Search the library computer database or card catalog for books or magazine articles with information on your topic.

4.

5.

6.

7. Make a time line, flowchart, or other graphic aid to show important information about the topic.

8.

Harcourt

SCHOOL-HOME CONNECTION With your child, write five questions you want to know the answers to. Use the library, bookstores, the Internet, or other people as resources to answer your questions.

Name _____

▶ As you read "Visitors from Space," complete the chart below. Fill in the first column with the story headings, the second column with questions about the headings, and the third column with answers to the questions.

Heading	Question	Review

▶ What is the Solar System, and what kind of scientists study it?

_____

_____

_____

TRY THIS! Draw the sun and the planets that surround it, each in its own orbit.

Harcourt

▶ **Read the passage about comets. Then fill in the "note cards" below. Follow the directions.**

Have you ever looked into the sky and thought you saw something that looked like a glowing lightbulb? You knew it wasn't a star, but you weren't sure what it was. Perhaps it was a comet.

Comets are made up of rock, dust, ice, and gas. They are dark until they get near the Sun. When a comet flies near the Sun, the icy parts in the comet reflect the Sun's light. Another reason comets glow is because of the gas in the coma part of the comet. That gas takes in sunlight.

▶ **Write a heading for this passage. Then write the main idea and the details.**

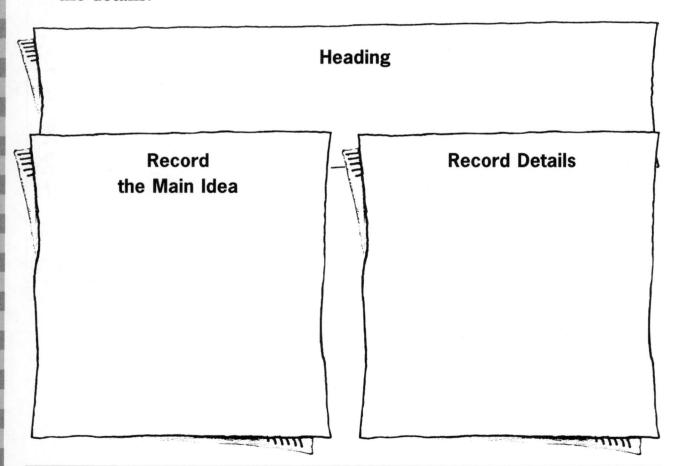

Heading

**Record
the Main Idea**

Record Details

**TRY
THIS!** On a sheet of paper, write the headings found in "Visitors from Space." Below each heading, write the main idea and some important details. Share your notes with a classmate.

Harcourt

Name _____

▶ **On the lines below, write the meaning of each underlined word in the paragraph. Then write the clue that helped you figure out the meaning.**

This <u>volcano</u> has not been active for many years. Still, the mountain could <u>erupt</u> at any time. Any <u>earthquake</u> activity could set it off. Such unusual earth movement could make molten rock, or <u>magma</u>, push to the surface. Once the magma comes out, it is called <u>lava</u>.

1. *Volcano* means _____.

2. Clue: _____

3. *Erupt* means _____.

4. Clue: _____

5. *Earthquake* means _____.

6. Clue: _____

7. *Magma* means _____.

8. Clue: _____

9. *Lava* means _____.

10. Clue: _____

TRY THIS! Look in a science book for at least three new words. Use clues to figure out the meanings. Then use each word in a sentence of your own.

Harcourt

Name _____

▶ **Rewrite each sentence, using the correct adverb in parentheses ( ).**

1. Does a comet burn **(hotter, hottest)** than a star?

_____

2. A comet moves **(more quickly, most quickly)** than an asteroid.

_____

3. Do comets glow **(more brightly, most brightly)** than the Moon?

_____

▶ **Fill in the blank, using the correct form of the adverb in parentheses ( ).**

4. The comet burned _____ than a wildfire. **(steadily)**

5. It glowed the _____ of all the objects. **(clearly)**

6. It appeared _____ than the Moon. **(high)**

7. It moved _____ than a planet would. **(quickly)**

8. It burned _____ of all the comets seen. **(long)**

TRY THIS!   Use *fast, faster,* and *fastest* in sentences comparing three comets.

Harcourt

Name _____

▶ **Write the Spelling Word that could replace the underlined word or words in each sentence.**

normal	simple	signal	total	middle

1. I never knew it was so <u>easy</u> to see a meteor shower.

_____

2. The <u>entire</u> number of meteors I've seen so far is sixteen.

_____

3. Is it <u>common</u> to see so many meteors? _____

4. I'm looking at the <u>center</u> of the sky. _____

5. I need to send a <u>noticeable message</u> to my mom. _____

▶ **Write the Spelling Word that best completes each sentence.**

title	purple	central

6. What is the _____ of your favorite book?

7. The family room is in the _____ part of our house.

8. My favorite color is _____.

Handwriting Tip: Make sure *le* does not look like *ee*. Write these words.

le

9. apple _____   **10.** able _____

SCHOOL-HOME CONNECTION With your child, walk around your neighborhood and identify things that end with *le* or *al*. For example, *people*, a *bottle*, a traffic *signal*, or a *purple* flower.

Harcourt

Skills and Strategies Index

COMPREHENSION

Cause and Effect 113–114, 120, 129
Characters' Feelings and Actions 48–49, 54, 63
Compare and Contrast 57–58, 64, 85
Fact and Opinion 21–22, 29, 38
Homographs and Homophones 4
Important Details 96–97, 102, 110
Paraphrase 88

Problem Solving 105, 121
Reality and Fantasy 28
Referents 123–124
Sequence 6–7, 12, 19
Summarize 66–67, 74, 84
Summarizing the Literature 5, 13, 20, 30, 39, 47, 56, 65, 76, 86, 95, 104, 112, 122, 131

GRAMMAR

Adjectives 9
   That Compare 42
   for *How Many* 25
   for *What Kind* 16
Adverbs 126
   Comparing with Adverbs 134
Articles 35
Contractions 117

Verbs
   Action Verbs 51
   Irregular Verbs 90
   Main and Helping Verbs 60
   More Irregular Verbs 99
   Past-Tense Verbs 80
   Present-Tense Verbs 71
   The Verb *Be* 107

LITERARY APPRECIATION

Author's Purpose 93

Figurative Language 31–32, 55, 94

SPELLING

Compound Words 52
Contractions *'s, 've, n't, 'd* 118
Homophones 17
Syllable Patterns
   VCCV Words 61
   VCV Words 72
Words in Which *y* Changes to *i*
   Before the Ending 108
Words That End Like
   little 135
   never 127

Words That End with
   -ed and *-ing* 81
   -tion and *-sion* 91
Words with
   Double Consonants 36
   -er and *-est* 43
   /ôr/ 10
   Suffixes *-er, -ful, -ly,* and *-able* 100
   /ûr/ 26

STUDY SKILLS

Book Parts 23, 103
Graphic Sources 68–69, 75, 83
Note-Taking Strategies 132
Reading Everyday Sources 33, 46, 87

Search Techniques 115, 130
Skim and Scan 40
Study Strategies 77, 111
Test-Taking Strategies 78

VOCABULARY

Analogies 24
Classifying 70
Clipped Words 89
Foreign Words 79
Gradient Analysis 34
Homographs 116
Homophones 8
Old-Fashioned Words 41
Onomatopoeia 15

Regional Words (southwest) 59
Related Words 98
Rhyming Words 125
Selection Vocabulary 3, 11, 18, 27, 37, 44, 53, 62, 73, 82, 92, 101, 109, 119, 128
Specialized Words 106, 133
Syllabication 14, 45
Vivid Verbs 50